Crochet Critters and Bugs

and Bugs

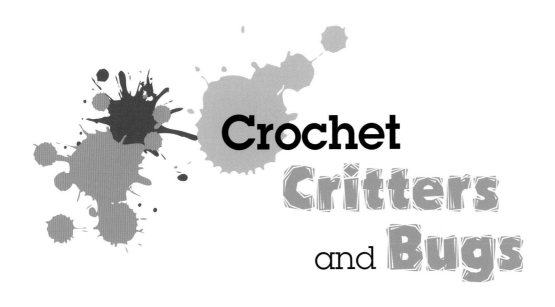

Crochet Critters and Bugs

STACKPOLE
BOOKS

Published by
STACKPOLE BOOKS
5067 Ritter Road
Mechanicsburg, PA 17055
www.stackpolebooks.com

Printed in U.S.A.

10 9 8 7 6 5 4 3 2 1

First edition

Cover design by Tessa J. Sweigert

Photos on pages 1 (except far left), 7, 8, 11 (bottom), 12, 16 (right), 17, 22 (bottom), 23, 28 (bottom right), 29, 32, 38 (bottom), 39, 41 (bottom), 43, 44, 52, 53, 54, 56 (bottom), 57, 60 (bottom left and right), 61, 64 (bottom), 65, 69, 70, 74, 75, 76, 81, 82, 87, 88, 91 (bottom), 92, 95 (middle right), 96, 100 (bottom left and right), 101, 103 (bottom), 104, 107 (right), 108, and 112 (top) by Tiffany Blackstone. All other photos are by the designers except where otherwise noted.

Library of Congress Cataloging-in-Publication Data

Crochet critters and bugs : 22 great projects. — First edition.
    pages cm
  Compiled by Kathryn L. Fulton.
  "These 22 patterns come from a number of talented designers and range from extra-realistic, life-size crochet sculptures to funny bug-eyed plushies and adorable amigurumi animals."
  Includes index.
  ISBN 978-0-8117-1252-1
1. Crocheting—Patterns. 2. Stuffed animals (Toys) I. Fulton, Kathryn, 1987– editor of compilation.
  TT829.C745 2014
  746.43'4—dc23
                        2013035332

Contents

About These Patterns

Crochet is a fun, creative, versatile craft—why stop with hats and sweaters? In this book you'll find patterns for unique, quirky creatures, from beloved classics like ladybugs and butterflies to more unusual animals such as tarantulas, jellyfish, and mosquitoes. These 22 patterns come from a number of talented designers and range from extra-realistic, life-size crochet sculptures to funny bug-eyed plushies and adorable amigurumi animals. Make them as gifts for kids (or kids at heart) or use them for some really unique décor!

Crocheting animals is, for the most part, like making any other project. However, a few special notes apply to the patterns in this book.

CROCHETING IN THE ROUND

Amigurumi and other stuffed projects are usually constructed by crocheting in the round. This saves you a lot of assembly time and results in a nicer-looking final project by eliminating the need for a side seam.

There are a number of ways to begin crocheting in the round. You can make a short chain (perhaps 4 or 5 stitches), then work a slip stitch in the first stitch of the chain to form a ring; work the stitches of the next row through the center of the ring instead of through the individual stitches of the chain. Another method of beginning in the round is to chain 2 and then work all the stitches for the first round in the second chain from the hook. When you begin the second round, spread out these closely-packed stitches of the first row/round into a circle and insert the hook into the first stitch of that row. You can also begin working in the round by making what is called a "magic ring"—an adjustable loop of yarn through which you make your first round of stitches. When the first round of stitches is complete, you pull on the tail of the loop to close the magic ring to tighten the loop to the perfect size for the number of stitches in it. You can easily find instructions and video tutorials for

making a magic ring, as well as for any other crochet technique, online. Each pattern will tell you which method to begin with—but it is possible to substitute one for another, if you have a method you prefer. Just make sure that you have the correct number of stitches at the end of the first round.

Most of the projects in this book use continuous rounds, meaning that the stitches are worked in a spiral, without any division between the end of one round and the beginning of the next. Because there is no clear beginning and end of the round in the work, you should always mark the beginning of your round with a stitch marker or a piece of scrap yarn. This is especially important when a pattern instructs you to repeat a certain group of stitches to the end of the round, without stating how many times to repeat them; marking rounds also allows you to check your work by counting the stitches after completing a round. Move the marker up to the end of a new round after completing each round. Unless a pattern specifically instructs you to join the end of the round to the beginning with a slip stitch, you should work in continuous rounds.

GAUGE

Most crochet books and patterns stress the importance of gauge—and rightly so. If you are making a sweater or pair of mittens that need to come out a particular size, making sure your crocheting matches what the pattern has in mind is essential to success. However, with amigurumi and other stuffed toys, the exact finished size is not very important. It doesn't have to fit a person, so an inch or two difference doesn't really matter.

For this reason, no gauge is given for any of the projects in this book. Finished measurements are included just to give you a general idea of the size of the piece, but your project may come out a little larger or smaller than the size given in the pattern, depending on the hook and yarn you choose. Alternatively, you might decide you want to make a much bigger or much smaller version of one of the projects—you can easily do this by going up or down a few yarn and hook sizes. The first project, the Giant Octopus, has an example of such a variation, but you could do the same with any project in the book.

What is important when crocheting any item that will be stuffed is that your work is tight enough that there will not be big gaps between the stitches for the stuffing to show through. For this reason, you will probably still want to crochet a test swatch with your chosen yarn and hook. Simply make a chain of 10 to 20 stitches and crochet several rows in single crochet (or, if the pattern mostly uses a different stitch, in that stitch); many of the patterns use single crochet through the back loop of each stitch, and it is a good idea to work your swatch in this way. When you have enough rows, wrap the swatch around some fiberfill, or stretch it out on a table with fiberfill underneath. If the stretched fabric is dense enough that there aren't too many gaps, then you are ready to start crocheting. If you have a lot of gaps, you may want to move down one or two hook sizes. If it was very difficult to get the hook into the work as you crocheted, or the finished fabric is very tight and stiff, you might want to use a larger hook.

ABBREVIATIONS AND YARN WEIGHTS

This book uses the Craft Yarn Council's standard abbreviations and yarn weight system. See page 113 for a list of abbreviations and page 115 for a chart with more information about yarn weights.

SEA LIFE

Giant Octopus

Designed by Kelly Lynn Smith • (https://www.facebook.com/AngelsunPatternDesigns) • Photos by Angelsun Photos

The octopus is a gentle giant of the ocean with a high I.Q. Although over 3 feet across, it can squeeze through an opening about the size of a quarter. This soft sculpture version only wants to squeeze into your heart.

With his long arms, this octopus is a master at giving gentle hugs. He will drape nicely over a couch back and makes an excellent bed companion. He can be made up very quickly in few hours on a large hook with super-bulky yarn.

YARN

6 Super Bulky

2 Fine

Super-bulky–weight chenile yarn in brown (for a large octopus it's important to use chenile yarn, as substitutions, even of the same weight, will not give the support necessary for such a big project)
Sport-weight flat chenile yarn in rust

HOOK

11.5 mm crochet hook

Note

This is an unusual hook size. If this size is not available, use the closest size possible that is appropriate to the yarn weight and will produce a semi-closed stitch.

NOTIONS

Two 30 mm black resin beads (for eyes)
Polyester fiberfill
Yarn needle

FINISHED MEASUREMENTS

42 inches long (from top of head to tip of tentacles);
53 inches wide (with tentacles spread out)

PATTERN

LEGS

With brown, ch 51.

Row 1: Sc in 2nd ch from hook and in next 9 chs, hdc in next 5 chs, dc in next 20 chs, hdc in next 7 chs, sc in next 8 chs.

Row 2: Turn, sl st in 2nd st from hook and in next 2 sts, sc in next 5 sts, hdc in next 8 sts, dc in next 7 sts, hdc in next 4 sts, sc in next 3 sts, sl st in next 2 sts.

Row 3: Turn, sl st in 2nd st from hook and in next 13 sts, sc in next 2 sts, hdc in next st, dc in next 5 sts, hdc in next st, sc in next 2 sts, sl st in next 6 sts.

Do not fasten off. Repeat foundation chain and rows 1–3 seven more times to make a total of 8 connected legs.

Round 1: Sl st in the base of the first leg to form a circle. Work 2 sc in the top of each leg around. (16 sts in round) Do not join, but continue around in a continous spiral.

Round 2: *Sc in next st, sc2tog. Rep from * around until the opening is closed (about 1 to 3 sts remaining, depending on yarn, hook size, and tension).

Fasten off and weave in end.

Sew the edges of each pair of legs together for 4 inches at the top.

Turn the down of the head down inside the neck. Sew in place, making sure to stitch through all layers, to make a firm neck.

HEAD

With brown, ch 24; sl st in first ch to form a ring.

Round 1: Sc in each ch around. (24 sts)

Round 2: Sc in each st around. (24 sts)

Short row 1 (neck shaping): Ch 1, turn. [Sc in next 2 sts, 2 sc in next st] 4 times. (16 sts)

Short row 2: Ch 1, turn. Sc in next 16 sts (back to original marker for beginning of row). (16 sts)

Round 3: Sc in each st around, skipping the turning chs and moving straight from the sts of round 2 to the higher sts of the neck rows. (28 sts)

Round 4: [Sc in next 2 sts, 2 sc in next st] 4 times, [sc 2, sc2tog] 4 times. (28 sts)

Round 5: Sc in next 14 sts, sc2tog twice, sc in next 6 sts, sc2tog twice. (24 sts)

Round 6: Sc in next 4 sts, 2 sc in each of next 4 sts, sc in next 16 sts. (28 sts)

Rounds 7–12: Sc in each st around. (28 sts)

Round 13: *Sc in next 5 sts, sc2tog; rep from * around. (24 sts)

Round 14: Sc in each st around. (24 sts)

Round 15: *Sc in next 4 sts, sc2tog; rep from * around. (22 sts)

Rounds 16–17: Sc in each st around. (22 sts)

Round 18: *Sc in next st, sc2tog; rep from * to last st, sc in last st. (15 sts)

Round 19: Sc in next st, *sc2tog, sc in next st; rep from * around. (11 sts)

Round 20: Sc2tog around until the opening is closed. Fasten off and weave in end.

FINISHING

Lightly stuff the head. It should be a bit wobbly. (If desired, you can place the fiberfill in a piece of pantyhose so it's not so white and noticeable through the gaps in the crocheted fabric.) Place the head on the neck with a bit of a tilt so that the head leans toward the back. Center the head so it is facing out between two legs. Sew in place.

The head shaping naturally forms the eye socket but it needs to be emphasized a bit. Secure a thread at the edge of one of the eye sockets. Pinch up the eye socket section and stitch around in a circle. Pull on the thread slightly so that the edge closes about halfway; tie off and weave in ends. Repeat for the other socket.

Reach inside the head and push one of the beads through the back of the eye opening. (Alternately, you may first place the bead in the eye socket and then pull the thread to tighten the opening.) The large stitches have plenty of stretch, so you should not have a problem "popping" the eye into place.

Turn the bead so that the hole is horizontal in the socket; the eye should appear to be staring straight ahead. Sew the bead into place with either matching yarn or thread (whatever works with the size of the hole in the bead).

Repeat the process for the other eye.

LEG INSERTS (MAKE 8)

With 2 strands of rust, ch 2.

Row 1: Sc in 2nd chain from hook. (1 st)

Row 2: Ch 1, turn. Work 2 sc in next st. (2 sts)

Row 3: Ch 1, turn. Sc in each st across. (2 sts)

Row 4: Ch 1, turn. 2 sc in each of next 2 sts. (4 sts)

Row 5: Repeat row 3. (4 sts)

Row 6: Ch 1, turn. 2 sc in next st, sc in next 2 sts, 2 sc in last st. (6 sts)

Row 7: Repeat row 3. (6 sts)

Row 8: Ch 1, turn. 2 sc in next st, sc in next 4 sts, 2 sc in last st. (8 sts)

Rows 9–10: Repeat row 3. (8 sts)

Row 11: Ch 2, turn. Dc in first st, hdc in next st, sc in next st, sl st 2 tog, sc in next st, hdc in next st, dc in last st. (7 sts)

Row 12: Ch 2, turn. Dc in first st, [sl st 2 tog] 3 times, dc in last st (same st as 2nd st of final sl st 2 tog). (5 sts)

Fasten off, leaving a long tail for sewing.

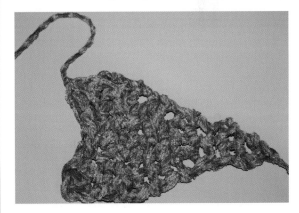

Place a triangular inset between a pair of legs, with the narrow, pointed end toward the top. Whipstitch in place on the wrong side, stretching the end (the long edge of webbing between the two legs) slightly.

Repeat with other 7 insets.

SIPHON

With brown, ch 7. Sl st in first ch to form a ring.
Round 1: 7 sc through ring. (7 sts)

Note

To eliminate an unsightly end that needs to be woven in, work the scs of round 1 around the tail of yarn from the beginning of the foundation chain.

Rounds 2–3: Sc in each st around. (7 sts)
Fasten off.
Sew the siphon to the right side of the octopus's head, at about the level of the eyes.

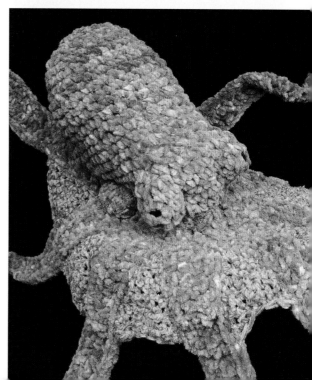

Mini Variation

Change the yarn weight and hook size to create a
miniature octopus. The one pictured at right was made
on a size G-6 (4.25 mm) hook with bulky yarn for the
body and medium-weight baby yarn for the inserts.
This delicate little octopus measures 22 inches across.

Nudibranch

Designed by CAROCreated/Carola Herbst • (http://www.etsy.com/de/shop/CAROcreated)

Nudibranchs, or sea slugs, are shell-less marine gastropods found in oceans worldwide. They range in adult size from ¼ inch to 2 feet. Some of the most colorful creatures on earth belong to this group. This project is a great way to use up small amounts of bright-colored lightweight yarn.

2 Fine

YARN
Sport-weight cotton-acrylic blend yarn in white, black, blue, orange, and yellow

HOOK
2.5 mm crochet hook

NOTIONS
Yarn needle
Stitch marker
Polyester fiberfill
Pins

FINISHED MEASUREMENTS
8 inches long; 3 inches wide

SPECIAL STITCH

Half treble crochet (htr): Yo twice. Insert hook into indicated stitch and draw up a loop (4 loops on hook). Yo and pull through 2 loops (3 loops on hook). Yo and pull through all remaining loops (1 loop on hook).

PATTERN

TOP OF BODY

With black, ch 25.

Round 1: Sc in 2nd ch from hook and in next ch, sl st in next 4 chs, sc in next 3 chs, hdc in next ch, dc in next 2 chs, hdc in next ch, sc in next 10 chs, 4 sc in last ch; continue around onto the bottom edge of the foundation chain, working in the unused loops: sc in next 9 chs, hdc in next 2 chs, dc in next 3 chs, hdc in next 2 chs, dc in next 2 chs, sl st in next 3 chs, sc in next ch, 3 sc in last ch, changing to blue in last sc (CC1). (52 sts) Do not break off black.

Round 2: With blue, sc in next 2 sts, hdc in next 4 sts, sc in next 4 sts, sl st in next 2 sts, sc in next 12 sts, 2 sc in each of next 2 sts, sc in next 12 sts, sl st in next 3 sts, sc in next 4 sts, hdc in next 3 sts, sc in next 2 sts, 2 sc in next st; change to black (CC2) and work 2 sc in last st. (56 sts) Do not break off blue.

Round 3: With black, sc in first st, changing to blue (CC1); with blue, sc in next 24 sts, 2 sc in each of next 2 sts, sc in next 26 sts, 2 sc in next st, sc in next st, changing to black (CC1); with black, sc in the same st again, sc in last st. (60 sts)

Round 4: With black, sc in first st, hdc in next st, 2 dc in next st, dc in next 3 sts, hdc in next st, dc in next 4 sts,

hdc in next 4 sts, sc in next 10 sts, 2 sc in next st, sc in next 2 sts, 2 sc in next st, sc in next 8 sts, hdc in next 4 sts, dc in next 5 sts, hdc in next 2 sts, dc in next 3 sts, 2 dc in next st, hdc in next st, [sc in next 2 sts, 2 sc in next st] twice, sc in last st. (66 sts)

Round 5: *Sc in next 27 sts, 2 sc in next st, sc in next 2 sts, 2 sc in next st, sc in next 2 sts; rep from * around, changing to white (CC1) in the last st. (70 sts)

Round 6: With white, *sc in next 26 sts, 2 sc in next st, sc in next 3 sts, 2 sc in next st, sc in next 2 sts, 2 sc in next st, sc in next st; rep from * around. (76 sts)

Set this piece aside while you crochet the underside of the body, but do not fasten off.

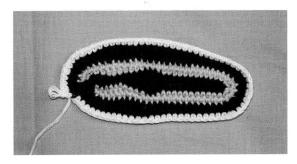

UNDERSIDE OF BODY

With blue, ch 31.

Round 1: Sc in 2nd ch from hook and next 28 chs, 4 sc in last ch; continue around onto the bottom edge of the foundation chain, working in the unused loops: sc in next 28 sts, 3 sc in last ch. (64 sts)

Round 2: *Sc in next 30 sts, 2 sc in each of next 2 sts; rep from * around. (68 sts)

Round 3: *Sc in next 30 sts, 2 sc in next st, sc in next 2 sts, 2 sc in next st; rep from * around. (72 sts)

Round 4: *Sc in next 31 sts, 2 sc in next st, sc in next 2 sts, 2 sc in next st; rep from * around. (76 sts)

Rounds 5–7: Sc in each st around. (76 sts)

Fasten off. Weave in all loose ends.

APPENDAGE (MAKE 8)

With orange, start with a magic ring.

Round 1: Ch 1, 3 sc in ring. (3 sts)

Round 2: 2 sc in first st, sc in next 2 sts. (4 sts)

Rounds 3–6: Sc in each st around. (4 sts)

Sl st in next st to even out end of round. Fasten off, leaving a long tail to use later to sew the appendage to the body.

ANTENNAE (MAKE 2)

With orange, start with a magic ring.

Round 1: Ch 1, 3 sc in ring. (3 sts)

Round 2: 2 sc in first st, sc in next 2 sts. (4 sts)

Round 3: Sc in each st around. (4 sts)

Round 4: 2 sc in first st, sc in next 3 sts. (5 sts)

Round 5: Sc in each st around. (5 sts)

Round 6: 2 sc in first st, sc in next 4 sts. (6 sts)

Rounds 7–12: Sc in each st around. (6 sts)

Sl st in next st to even out end of round. Fasten off, leaving a long tail to use later to sew the appendage to the body.

ASSEMBLING THE BODY AND CROCHETING THE RUFFLE

Sew the two antennae and the eight appendages onto the upper side of the body, using the long tails left when fastening the pieces off. Use the photo below as a guide.

Allign the top and bottom of the body with right sides facing out, making sure to line up the center lines of the pieces. Pick up the white yarn from the top and work around the body as described in round 1, crocheting through both the next stitch of the top and the corresponding stitch of the underside for every stitch. Stop several stitches before the end of round 1 to stuff the body firmly, then finish the round.

Round 1: *2 sc in next st, sc in next st; rep from * to end of round. (114 sts)

Fasten off. Weave in ends.

Join yellow anywhere in round 1.

Round 2: Ch 1, sc in same st as joining, sc in each st around. (114 sts)

Round 3: *2 sc in next st, sc in next st; rep from * around. (171 sts)

Count to find the back center st and mark this stitch with a stitch marker.

Round 4: Sc in each st to 2 sts before marker, hdc in next st, dc in next st; remove marker from next st and htr in this stitch, replace marker in newly formed htr; dc in next st, hdc in next st, sc in each st to end of round. (171 sts)

Fasten off. Weave in ends.

Join white anywhere in round 4.

Round 5: *2 sc in next st, sc in next st**; rep from * to ** until 3 sts before marker, hdc in next 2 sts, dc in next st; remove marker from next st and work 3 htr in this stitch; dc in next st, hdc in next 2 sts; rep from * to ** to end of round.

Fasten off. Weave in ends.

TAIL

With blue, start with a magic ring.

Round 1: Ch 1, 5 sc in ring. (5 sts)

Round 2: 2 sc in first st, sc in next 4 sts. (6 sts)

Round 3: Sc in next st, 2 sc in next st, sc in next 4 sts. (7 sts)

Round 4: Sc in next st, 2 sc in each of next 2 sts, sc in next 2 sts, sc2tog. (8 sts)

Round 5: Sc in next 2 sts, 2 sc in next st, 5 sc in next st. (9 sts)

Note: From this point on the decreases (sc2tog) will always be between the last stitch of the current round and the first stitch of the next round. Work the decrease as you normally would, then count the next stitch after the decrease as the first stitch of the new round.

Round 6: Sc in next 3 sts, 2 sc in each of next 2 sts, sc in next 3 sts, sc2tog. (11 sts)

Round 7: Sc in next 3 sts, 2 sc in next st, sc in next 6 sts. (11 sts)

Round 8: Sc in next 4 sts, 2 sc in each of next 2 sts, sc in next 4 sts, sc2tog. (13 sts)

Round 9: Sc in next 4 sts, 2 sc in next st, sc in next 7 sts. (13 sts)

Round 10: Sc in next 5 sts, 2 sc in each of next 2 sts, sc in next 5 sts, sc2tog. (15 sts)

Round 11: Sc in next 5 sts, 2 sc in next st, sc in next 8 sts. (15 sts)

Round 12: Sc in next 6 sts, 2 sc in each of next 2 sts, sc in next 6 sts, sc2tog. (17 sts)

Round 13: Sc in next 6 sts, 2 sc in next st, sc in next 9 sts. (17 sts)

Sl st in next st to even out end of round. Fasten off, leaving a long tail to use when sewing the appendage to the body.

Stuff the tail (but do not overstuff).

Pin the tail to the underside of the body, in the center on the back end. Sew both pieces together with the long tail left from fastening off.

Jellyfish

Designed by Wendy Thornburg • (http://www.drunkenauntwendydesigns.wordpress.com)

This project has all the whimsy of a jellyfish without the annoying sting! Crochet is the perfect technique for creating curly tentacles—they are easy to make but look impressive. In worsted-weight yarn, this jellyfish comes out about 2 feet long; for a smaller jelly, try a smaller yarn-hook combo.

YARN

Worsted-weight yarn in aqua (MC) and light peach (CC)

I originally used Nightlights Glow-in-the-Dark Yarn for the CC. If you can find some of this, the cool effect it gives is definitely worth it.

HOOKS

Size E-4 (3.5 mm) crochet hook
Size G-6 (4 mm) crochet hook

NOTIONS

Yarn needle
Polyester fiberfill

FINISHED MEASUREMENTS

23 inches long; body 29 inches around

PATTERN

BODY

With size E hook and MC, ch 2.

Round 1: Work 6 sc in second ch from hook.

Round 2: Starting in the first sc of round 1 (to work in round in a continuous spiral), work 2 sc in each st. (12 sts)

Round 3: *Sc in next st, 2 sc in next st; rep from * around. (18 sts)

Round 4: *Sc in next 2 sts, 2 sc in next st; rep from * around. (24 sts) Change to CC in last st.

Round 5: *Sc in next 3 sts, 2 sc in next st; rep from * around. (30 sts) Change to MC in last st.

Round 6: *Sc in next 4 sts, 2 sc in next st; rep from * around. (36 sts)

Round 7: *Sc in next 5 sts, 2 sc in next st; rep from * around. (42 sts)

Round 8: *Sc in next 6 sts, 2 sc in next st; rep from * around. (48 sts)

Round 9: *Sc in next 7 sts, 2 sc in next st; rep from * around. (54 sts) Change to CC in last st.

Round 10: *Sc in next 8 sts, 2 sc in next st; rep from * around. (60 sts)

Round 11: *Sc in next 9 sts, 2 sc in next st; rep from * around. (66 sts) Change to MC in last st.

Round 12: *Sc in next 10 sts, 2 sc in next st; rep from * around. (72 sts)

Round 13: *Sc in next 11 sts, 2 sc in next st; rep from * around. (78 sts)

Round 14: *Sc in next 12 sts, 2 sc in next st; rep from * around. (84 sts)

Rounds 15 and 16: Sc in each st around.

Switch to size G hook and add in CC. Continue, holding both colors together.

Rounds 17–20: Sc in each st around.

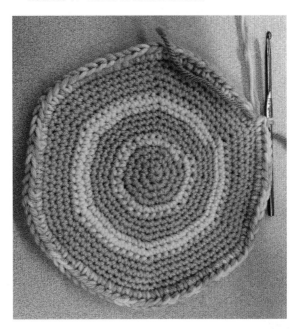

Round 21: *Sc in next 12 sts, sc2tog; rep from * around. (78 sts)

Round 22: *Sc in next 11 sts, sc2tog; rep from * around. (72 sts)

Rounds 23–26: Sc in each st around.

Switch to size E hook. Drop CC and continue with MC only.

Rounds 27–28: Sc in each st around.

Round 29: *Sc in next 10 sts, sc2tog; rep from * around. (66 sts)

Round 30: *Sc in next 9 sts, sc2tog; rep from * around. (60 sts)

Round 31: *Sc in next 8 sts, sc2tog; rep from * around. (54 sts)

Round 32: *Sc in next 7 sts, sc2tog; rep from * around. (48 sts)

Round 33: *Sc in next 6 sts, sc2tog; rep from * around. (42 sts)

Round 34: *Sc in next 5 sts, sc2tog; rep from * around. (36 sts)

Round 35: *Sc in next 4 sts, sc2tog; rep from * around. (30 sts)

Round 36: *Sc in next 3 sts, sc2tog; rep from * around. (24 sts)

Round 37: Sc tbl in each st around. Stuff the portion of the jellyfish already completed and continue to add stuffing every few rows through the end of the body.

Rounds 38–40: Sc in each st around.

Round 41: *Sc in next 3 sts, 2 sc in next st; rep from * around. (30 sts)

Round 42: *Sc in next 4 sts, 2 sc in next st; rep from * around. (36 sts)

Round 43: *Sc in next 5 sts, 2 sc in next st; rep from * around. (42 sts)

Rounds 44–47: Sc in each st around.

Round 48: *Sc in next 5 sts, sc2tog; rep from * around. (36 sts)

Round 49: *Sc in next 4 sts, sc2tog; rep from * around. (30 sts)

Round 50: *Sc in next 3 sts, sc2tog; rep from * around. (24 sts)

Round 51: *Sc in next 2 sts, sc2tog; rep from * around. (18 sts)

Round 52: *Sc in next st, sc2tog; rep from * around. (12 sts)

Round 53: Sc2tog around. (6 sts)

Fasten off, leaving a long tail. Thread tail through last six sts and pull up tight to close opening.

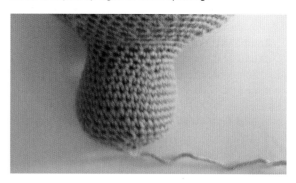

SKIRT

Note this part is not worked flat in rows, not in the round.

With size G hook and CC, ch 61.

Row 1: Sc in second ch from hook and in each ch across. Turn. (60 sts)

Row 2: Ch 1, work 2 sc in each st across. Turn. (120 sts)

Row 3: Repeat row 2. (240 sts)

Row 4: Repeat row 2. (480 sts)

Row 5: Ch 1, sc in each st across.

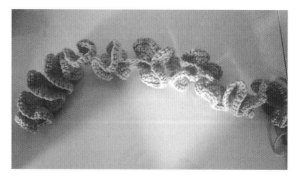

Fasten off. Sew the foundation chain to the body along the bottom of the multicolored section. It helps to pin this skirt in place before sewing to make sure you have the placement and stretch of the piece correct.

TENTACLES

You can make as many tentacles as you want in any color combination. To match the sample, make five with two strands of CC and two with both colors held together.

With size G hook, ch 51.

Row 1: Sc in second ch from hook and in each ch across. Turn. (50 sts)

Row 2: Ch 1, work 2 sc in each st across. (100 sts)

Sew one CC tentacle to the very bottom of the body, where you sewed the hole closed. Flank it with the two multicolored tentacles. Sew the remaining four tentacles to the bottom of the body, beneath the skirt.

FINISHING
Weave in all ends. Thread a few pieces of yarn through the very top of the jellyfish to create a loop for hanging the project.

Crab

Designed by Katie Christy • *(http://www.etsy.com/shop/Yarnington)*

This charming little crab comes with an egg to hide inside and makes a great toy for a young child. (If you make it for a baby or toddler, be sure to embroider the eyes instead of using beads or buttons, which are a choking hazard.) Of course, real-life crab eggs are clearish rather than white, and not nearly as large as this one—but real-life crabs aren't nearly as cute as this crocheted version!

4
Medium

YARN
Worsted-weight yarn in bright orange

HOOK
Size F-5 (3.75 mm) crochet hook

NOTIONS
Stitch marker
Embroidery needle
Embroidery floss, beads, or buttons for eyes
Embroidery floss for mouth
Polyester fiberfill

FINISHED MEASUREMENTS
crab 2$\frac{1}{2}$ inches tall; egg 4$\frac{1}{2}$ inches tall

PATTERN

CRAB

Start with a magic ring.

Round 1: Work 6 sc in magic ring. (6 sts)

Round 2: 2 sc in each st around. (12 sts)

Round 3: *2 sc in next st, sc in next st; rep from * around. (18 sts)

Round 4: *2 sc in next st, sc in next 2 sts; rep from * around. (24 sts)

Round 5: *2 sc in next st, sc in next 3 sts; rep from * around. (30 sts)

Rounds 6–8: Sc in each st around.

Round 9: Sc in next 4 sts, work claw 1 (see below), sc in next 20 sts, work claw 2 (see below), sc in next 4 sts.

Claw 1: Sc in next st, ch 8 (arm formed), work 4 sc in 2nd ch from hook.

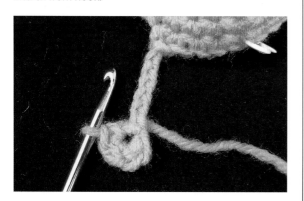

Now work in the round in these 4 sts: [2 sc in first st, sc in next st, 2 sc in next st, sc in last st].

Proceed in rows:

Row 1: Ch 1, turn, sc2tog, sc in next 2 sts, sc2tog. (4 sts)

Row 2: Ch 1, turn, sc2tog twice. (2 sts)

Row 3: Ch 1, turn, sc2tog. (1 st)

Row 4: Ch 1, *do not turn*, sc down the side of the claw (4 sts), sc into the middle st at the base of the claw. Ch 3, sl st in the 2nd ch from the hook, sc in next ch, sl st in the middle st at the base of the claw.

Sl st down the arm chain, sl st in the sc at the very beginning of the claw.

Claw 2: Sc in next st, ch 8 (arm formed), work 4 sc in 2nd ch from hook.

Now work in the round in these 4 sts: [2 sc in first st, sc in next st, 2 sc in next st, sc in last st]. Proceed in rows:

Row 1: Ch 1, turn, sc2tog, sc in next 2 sts, sc2tog. (4 sts)

Row 2: Ch 1, turn, sc2tog twice. (2 sts)

Row 3: Ch 1, turn, sc2tog. (1 st)

Row 4: Ch 1, *turn,* sc down the side of the claw (4 sts), sc into the middle st at the base of the claw. Ch 3, sl st in the 2nd ch from the hook, sc in next ch, sl st in the middle st at the base of the claw.

Sl st down the arm chain, sl st in the sc at the very beginning of the claw.

One claw points down, the other to the side, for a whimsical look. To have them exactly the same, you can make one arm/claw combo independently and sew it onto the body.

Round 10: Sc in next 5 sts, sk next ch and sl st, sc in next 21 sts, sk next ch and sl st, sc in next 4 sts. (30 sts)

Round 11: *Sc2tog, sc in next 3 sts; rep from * around. (24 sts)

Round 12: Sc in next 3 sts, work leg (see next page) 4 times, sc in next 4 sts, work leg 4 times, sc in next st. (24 sts)

Leg: Sc in next st, ch 3, hdc in 2nd ch from hook, sc in next ch, sl st in beginning sc, sc in next st.

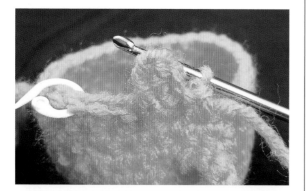

Round 13: *Sc2tog, sc in next 2 sc; rep from * around, skipping all chs and sl sts. (18 sts) Attach eyes and embroider mouth.

Round 14: *Sc2tog, sc in next st; rep from * around. (12 sts) Stuff somewhat firmly.

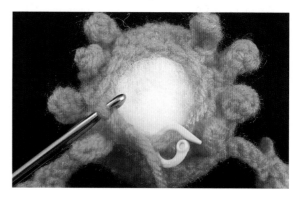

Round 15: Sc2tog around. (6 sts)
Fasten off, leaving a long tail. Weave tail through rem 6 sts, pull closed, and fasten off. Weave in end.

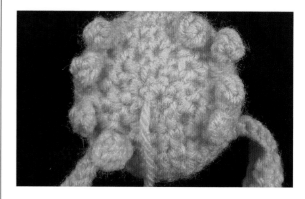

EGG
Top
Start with a magic ring.
Round 1: Work 6 sc in magic ring; join with sl st in beg sc. (6 sts)
Round 2: Ch 1, 2 sc in each st around; join with sl st in beg ch. (12 sts)
Round 3: Ch 1, *2 sc in next st, sc in next st; rep from * around; join with sl st in beg ch. (18 sts)
Round 4: Ch 1, *2 sc in next st, sc in next 2 sts; rep from * around; join with sl st in beg ch. (24 sts)
Round 5: Ch 1, sc in each st around; join with sl st in beg ch. (24 sts)

Round 6: Ch 1, *2 sc in next st, sc in next 3 sts; rep from * around; join with sl st in beg ch. (30 sts)

Rounds 7–8: Ch 1, sc in each st around; join with sl st in beg ch. (30 sts)

Round 9: Ch 1, *2 sc in next st, sc in next 4 sts; rep from * around; join with sl st in beg ch. (36 sts)

Rounds 10–14: Ch 1, sc in each st around; join with sl st in beg ch. (36 sts)

Round 15: Ch 1, sc tbl in each st around; join with sl st in beg ch. (36 sts)

Round 16: Ch 1, sc in next 18 sts, sc2tog, sc in each st to end of round; join with sl st in beg ch. (35 sts)

Now proceed in a continuous spiral, without joining at the end of each round.

Rounds 17–19: Sc in each st around. (35 sts)

Round 20: *Sc2tog, sc in next 4 sts; rep from * to last 5 sts, sc2tog, sc in next 3 sts. (29 sts)

Rounds 21–22: Sc in each st around. (29 sts)

Round 23: *Sc2tog, sc in next 3 sts; rep from * to last 4 sts, sc2tog, sc in next 2 sts. (23 sts)

Round 24: Sc in each st around. (23 sts)

Round 25: *Sc2tog, sc in next 2 sts; rep from * to last 3 sts, sc2tog, sc in next st. (17 sts)

Round 26: *Sc2tog, sc in next st; rep from * to last 2 sts, sc2tog. (11 sts)

Round 27: Sc2tog 5 times.

Fasten off, leaving a long tail. Weave tail through rem sts, pull up tightly, and fasten off.

Turn the top half of the piece inside out along round 13 (the sc tbl round) so that it nests inside the bottom half of the piece to form a cup shape. Sew around the bottom through both layers to secure. Weave in end.

Bottom

Start with a magic ring.

Round 1: Work 6 sc in magic ring; join with sl st in beg sc. (6 sts)

Round 2: Ch 1, 2 sc in each st around; join with sl st in beg ch. (12 sts)

Round 3: Ch 1, *2 sc in next st, sc in next st; rep from * around; join with sl st in beg ch. (18 sts)

Round 4: Ch 1, *2 sc in next st, sc in next 2 sts; rep from * around; join with sl st in beg ch. (24 sts)

Round 5: Ch 1, *2 sc in next st, sc in next 3 sts; rep from * around; join with sl st in beg ch. (30 sts)

Rounds 6–7: Ch 1, sc in each st around; join with sl st in beg ch. (30 sts)

Round 8: Ch 1, *2 sc in next st, sc in next 4 sts; rep from * around; join with sl st in beg ch. (36 sts)

Rounds 9–12: Ch 1, sc in each st around; join with sl st in beg ch. (36 sts)

Round 13: Ch 1, sc tbl in each st around; join with sl st in beg ch. (36 sts)

Round 14: Ch 1, sc in next 18 sts, sc2tog, sc in each st to end of round; join with sl st in beg ch. (35 sts)

Now proceed in a continuous spiral, without joining at the end of each round.

Rounds 15–16: Sc in each st around. (35 sts)

Round 17: *Sc2tog, sc in next 4 sts; rep from * to last 5 sts, sc2tog, sc in next 3 sts. (29 sts)

Round 18: Sc in each st around. (29 sts)

Round 19: *Sc2tog, sc in next 3 sts; rep from * to last 4 sts, sc2tog, sc in next 2 sts. (23 sts)

Round 20: *Sc2tog, sc in next 2 sts; rep from * to last 3 sts, sc2tog, sc in next st. (17 sts)

Round 21: *Sc2tog, sc in next st; rep from * to last 2 sts, sc2tog. (11 sts)

Round 22: Sc2tog 5 times.

Fasten off, leaving a long tail. Weave tail through rem sts, pull up tightly, and fasten off.

Finish as for top of egg.

FINISHING

Sew edges of top and bottom of egg together over about half an inch. Weave in ends.

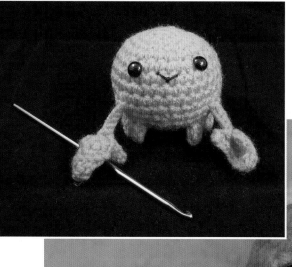

Pygmy Seahorse

Designed by Kelly Lynn Smith • (https://www.facebook.com/AngelsunPatternDesigns) • Photos by Angelsun Photos

At 4³/₄ inches, this crocheted pygmy seahorse is larger than her real-world counterpart, who is no larger than 1 inch. *Hippocampus bargibanti* was discovered in 1969, after hitching a ride on a gorgonian (an underwater creature similar to coral). Typical of this species, our seahorse is yellow (their colors also range to a coral or pink shade), has a short, bulbous snout, and is covered in knobby tubercles. She is clinging to a bit of seafan with the same type of tubercles, where she remains camouflaged.

1 Super Fine

YARN
Fingering-weight yarn in yellow

HOOK
Size E-4 (3.5 mm) crochet hook

NOTIONS
E-6000 glue
16" strand of round yellow jade beads, 4 mm in diameter
Pair of 8 mm light amber glass eyes
Polyester fiberfill
Sewing needle
Thread to match yarn

FINISHED MEASUREMENTS
5 inches tall (not counting plant)

PATTERN

BODY

With two strands of yarn, ch 5, sl st in first ch to form a ring.

Round 1: Work 7 sc in ring. (7 sts)

Break off one strand of yarn and continue with rem strand.

Round 2: Sc in next st, sc2tog, sc in next 4 sts. (6 sts)

Rounds 3–4: Sc in each st around. (6 sts)

Round 5: *Sc in next st, 2 sc in next st; rep from * around. (9 sts)

Round 6: *Sc in next 2 sts, 2 sc in next st; rep from * around. (12 sts)

Round 7: *Sc in next 3 sts, 2 sc in next st; rep from * around. (15 sts)

Rounds 8–9: Sc in each st around. (15 sts)

Round 10: Sc in next 2 sts, 2 sc in next st, sc in next 3 sts, ch 2, sc in 2nd ch from hook (bump 1 made), sc in next 4 sts, ch 2, sc in 2nd ch from hook (bump 2 made), sc in next 3 sts, 2 sc in next st, sc in last st. (17 sts, not counting bumps)

Round 11: Sc in next 7 sts, skip ch and sc of bump 1 (working behind bump), sc in next 2 sts, ch 3, sc in 2nd ch from hook, hdc in next ch, sk next sc, sc in next st, skip ch and sc of bump 2 (working behind bump), sc in next 6 sts. (16 sts)

Round 12: Sc in next 9 sts, sc in skipped st of round 11, sc in next 7 sts. (17 sts)

Round 13: Sc in next 3 sts, sc2tog, sc in next 4 sts, sc2tog, sc in next 3 sts, sc2tog, sc in last st. (14 sts)

Round 14 (beginning of neck): Sc in next 3 sts, sc2tog, sc in next 3 sts, hdc in next 4 sts, sc2tog. (12 sts)

Round 15: Sc in next 6 sts, hdc in next st, 2 hdc in each of next 2 sts, hdc in next st, sc in next 2 sts. (14 sts)

Round 16: Sc in next st, sc2tog, sc in next 3 sts, hdc in next 6 sts, sc in next 2 sts. (13 sts)

Stuff head before continuing.

Round 17: Sc in next st, sc2tog, sc in next 3 sts, hdc in next st, sc in next 2 sts. (12 sts)

Round 18: Sc in next 5 sts, hdc in next 5 sts, sc in next 2 sts. (12 sts)

Round 19: Sc2tog, sc in next 3 sts, hdc in next 5 sts, sc in next 2 sts. (11 sts)

Round 20: Sc in next 5 sts, hdc in next 4 sts, sc in next 2 sts. (11 sts)

Rounds 21–24: Sc in each st around. (11 sts)

Stuff neck. Stitch the chin and the neck together to hold head down in position.

Round 25: Sc in next 3 sts, 2 sc in each of next 3 sts, sc in next 5 sts. (14 sts)

Round 26: Sc in next 6 sts, 2 sc in next st, sc in next 7 sts. (15 sts)

Round 27: Sc2tog, sc in next 3 sts, 2 sc in each of next 5 sts, sc in next 3 sts, sc2tog. (18 sts)

Rounds 28–29: Sc in each st around. (18 sts)

Round 30: Sc in next 9 sts, 2 sc in next st, sc in next st, 2 sc in next st, sc in next 6 sts. (20 sts)

Round 31: Sc in each st around. (20 sts)

Round 32: Sc in next 10 sts, 2 sc in next st, sc in next st, 2 sc in next st, sc in next 7 sts. (22 sts)

Rounds 33–34: Sc in each st around. (22 sts)

Stuff belly.

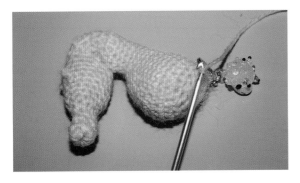

Round 35: Sc in next 10 sts, [sc2tog, sc in next st] 3 times, sc in next 3 sts. (19 sts)

Round 36: Sc in next 7 sts, [sc2tog, sc in next st, sc2tog] twice, sc in next 2 sts. (15 sts)

Round 37: Sc in next 9 sts, sc2tog twice, sc in next 2 sts. (13 sts)

Add more stuffing to body as needed.

Round 38: Sc in next 3 sts, sc2tog, sc in next 3 sts, sc2tog, sc in next st, sc2tog. (10 sts)

Round 39 (beginning of tail): Sc in next 6 sts, sc2tog twice. (8 sts)

Rounds 40–45: Sc in each st around. (8 sts)

Round 46: Sc in next 3 sts, sc2tog, sc in next 3 sts. (7 sts)

Rounds 47–50: Sc in each st around.

Tail should measure $1^1/_2$ inches from round 38 at this point; if the length is wrong, add or pull out rounds of straight single crochet until the tail is the correct length.

Round 51: Sc in next 2 sts, sc2tog, sc in next 3 sts. (6 sts)

Twist two pipe cleaners together to measure $4^1/_4$ inches. Insert into body until only $1^1/_2$ inches of the twist extends out the end of the tail.

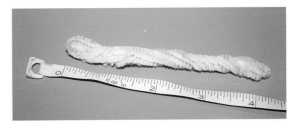

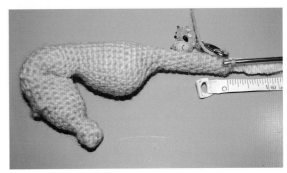

Round 52: Sc in each st around. (6 sts)

Repeat round 52 until the end of the pipe cleaner twist is covered.

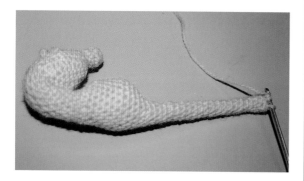

Final round: Sc2tog 3 times.

Fasten off and weave in end.

FIN

Ch 6.

Row 1: Sc in 2nd ch from hook and in each ch across. Ch 1, turn. (5 sts)

Row 2: Work 2 sc in each of next 2 sts, sc in next st, 2 sc in each of next 2 sts. Ch 2, turn. (9 sts)

Row 3: Hdc in each st across. (9 sts)

Fasten off; weave in end.

PLANT

First frond: Ch 15; sc in 2nd ch from hook and in each ch across. (14 sts)

Second frond: Continuing from the end of the first frond without fastening off, ch 18. Sc in 2nd ch from hook and in next 16 chs. (17 sts)

Third frond: Continuing from the end of the second frond without fastening off, ch 21. Sc in 2nd ch from hook in in next 19 chs. (20 sts)

Fold all three fronds together and insert the hook in the last stitch of each; sc through all 3 sts at once. Continue from here without fastening off.

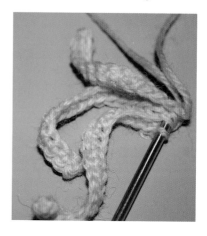

Stem: Ch 40. Hdc in 3rd ch from hook and in next 37 chs. (38 sts)

Edging: Sl st to base of stem to join. Continue along the edge of the stem as follows: *Ch 4, sc in 2nd ch from hook and next ch, hdc in next ch, sl st in next 3 sts along stem**; rep from * to ** along the length of the stem.

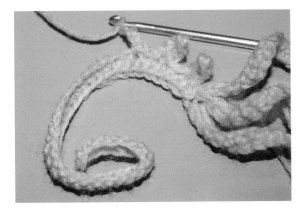

When you reach the end of the stem, work 3 sl st in last st, then turn piece to work along the other side of the stem. Sl st in next few sts until you are opposite the gap between two nodules on the opposite side.

Work from * to ** and repeat up the length of this side of the stem. Fasten off.

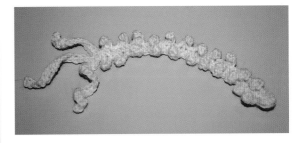

With the sewing needle and thread, sew a yellow bead to each nodule. Sew a few more beads randomly scattered across the plant.

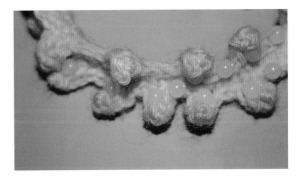

FINISHING
Sew the fin to the center of the back of the seahorse.

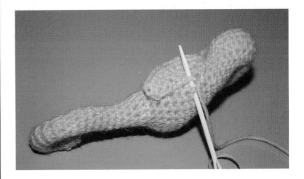

Clip the wire on the eyes so that it is around $1/2$ inch long. Test the fit on the seahorse's head.

Remove the eyes, noting where the center was. With yellow yarn, stitch two intersecting Xs over this center.

With sewing needle and thread, sew two beads at the top of the forehead and to each of the crocheted tubercles. Randomly sew beads to the remainder of the body. Then sew the plant to the seahorse as shown.

Use the E–6000 glue to attach the glass eyes in the center of the embroidered eye.

Clam

Designed by Stacey Trock • (http://www.freshstitches.com)

Not only is this little clam adorable . . . he's a puppet! This amigurumi is constructed so that you can stick your hand in his shell and even move around his eyes! If you aren't interested in a puppet, simply stuff him and stitch him closed in the back.

Medium

YARN
Worsted-weight yarn in tan (Color A—70 yards), pink (color B—20 yards), and black (color C—20 yards)

HOOK
Size G-6 (4 mm) crochet hook

NOTIONS
Yarn needle
12 mm blue animal eyes
Polyester fiberfill

FINISHED MEASUREMENTS
$4^1/_2$ inches wide

PATTERN

Note

Crochet through the back loop only throughout.

SHELL (MAKE 2)
With color A, ch 2.
Round 1: Work 6 sc in 2nd ch from hook. (6 sts)
Round 2: Starting with the first st of round 1 to work in the round, work 2 sc in each st around. (12 sts)

Round 3: *2 sc in next st, sc in next st; rep from * around. (18 sts)
Round 4: *2 sc in next st, sc in next 2 sts; rep from * around. (24 sts)
Round 5: *2 sc in next st, sc in next 3 sts; rep from * around. (30 sts)
Round 6: *2 sc in next st, sc in next 4 sts; rep from * around. (36 sts)
Round 7: *2 sc in next st, sc in next 5 sts; rep from * around. (42 sts)
Round 8: *2 sc in next st, sc in next 6 sts; rep from * around. (48 sts)
Rounds 9–10: Sc in each st around. (48 sts)
Round 11: *Sc2tog, sc in next 6 sts; rep from * around. (42 sts)
Rounds 12–13: Sc in each st around. (42 sts)
Round 14: *Sc2tog, sc in next 5 sts; rep from * around. (36 sts)
Rounds 15–16: Sc in each st around. (36 sts)
Round 17: *Sc2tog, sc in next 4 sts; rep from * around. (30 sts)
Rounds 18–19: Sc in each st around. (30 sts)

Fasten off, leaving a long tail.

TONGUE
With color B, ch 2.
Round 1: Work 6 sc in 2nd ch from hook. (6 sts)
Round 2: Starting with the first st of round 1 to work in the round, work 2 sc in each st around. (12 sts)
Round 3: *2 sc in next st, sc in next st; rep from * around. (18 sts)
Round 4: *2 sc in next st, sc in next 2 sts; rep from * around. (24 sts)
Round 5: *2 sc in next st, sc in next 3 sts; rep from * around. (30 sts)
Round 6: *2 sc in next st, sc in next 4 sts; rep from * around. (36 sts)
Rounds 7–8: Sc in each st around. (36 sts)
Round 9: *Sc2tog, sc in next 4 sts; rep from * around. (30 sts)
Rounds 10–11: Sc in each st around. (30 sts)
Round 12: *Sc2tog, sc in next 3 sts; rep from * around. (24 sts)
Rounds 13–14: Sc in each st around. (24 sts)
Fasten off.

EYESTALKS (MAKE 2)

With color C, ch 2.

Round 1: Work 6 sc in 2nd ch from hook. (6 sts)

Round 2: Starting with the first st of round 1 to work in the round, work 2 sc in each st around. (12 sts)

Rounds 3–13: Sc in each st around. (12 sts)

Fasten off.

Fasten eyes directly to the center of round 1, as pictured. To do so, insert post between desired stitches, and press washer onto back post to secure.

ASSEMBLY

When your clam puppet is completed, you will be able to stick your hand into both halves of the shell and insert your fingers into the eyestalks. Make sure that you don't close up these parts!

Let's start with the lower shell. Flatten the shell and make sure the long tail is on your right. The bottom edge of the opening will be left empty, and the top half is where you will attach the tongue and eyes. Flatten the tongue as well.

With the long tail, thread your tapestry needle through one stitch of the top edge of the shell opening, through the tongue, and through a stitch on the bottom

edge of an eye. Continue to do this until you have stitched through all of the stitches on the bottom of the eye. Continue for the second eye. Fasten off when completed.

The shell should be open so your hand can go in it, and the eyes only stitched through their bottoms (so you can slip a finger in each one).

Now attach the top half of the shell. Again, flatten the shell. Using the long tail, stitch the stitches on the bottom edge of the shell opening and the stitches on the top edges of the eyes together, as before. When completed, the back of your clam should look roughly like the photo here.

Weave in the ends, and you're finished!

As a puppet or a plushie, this little guy is a charmer!

Leafy Sea Dragon

Designed by Kelly Lynn Smith • (https://www.facebook.com/AngelsunPatternDesigns) • Photos by Angelsun Photos

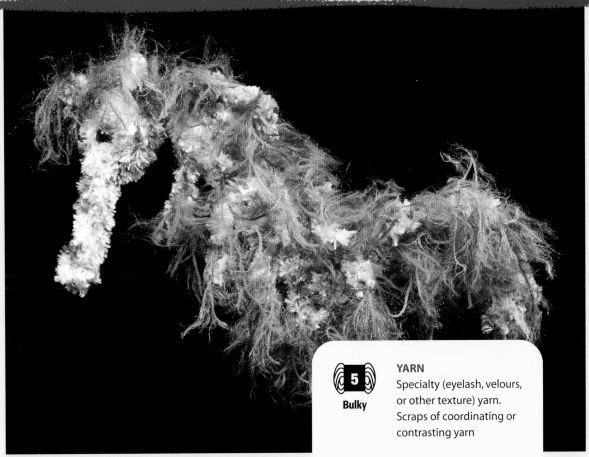

A relative of the seahorse, the sea dragon likes to hide among the leaves of kelp beds. Its appendages serve as camouflage in its native habitat along the southern and western coasts of Australia. Popularly known as "leafies," sea dragons are the marine emblem of the state of South Australia. They are fully mature at two years of age and grow to 18 inches long. This crocheted version is true to scale.

5
Bulky

YARN
Specialty (eyelash, velours, or other texture) yarn. Scraps of coordinating or contrasting yarn

HOOK
Size H-8 (5.0 mm) crochet hook

NOTIONS
E-6000 glue
Pair of 12 mm amber glass eyes
Polyester fiberfill
Sewing needle
2 white pipe cleaners
Yarn needle

FINISHED MEASUREMENTS
18 inches long

33

PATTERN

The sample shown in the step-by-step photos was made with regular yarn to make it easier to see the stitches. For a fluffy sea dragon like the one shown on page 33, use a novelty yarn such as eyelash yarn.

BODY

Ch 2.

Round 1: 5 sc in 2nd ch from hook. (5 sts)

Round 2: Starting in first sc of round 1 to work in the round in a continuous spiral, sc in each st around. (5 sts)

Rounds 3–12: Sc in each st around. (5 sts)

Round 13: Sc in first st, 2 sc in next st, sc in next st, 2 sc in next st, sc in last st. (7 sts)

Round 14: 2 sc in each st around. (14 sts)

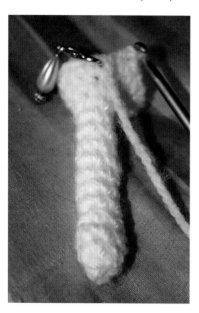

Rounds 15–20: Sc in each st around. (14 sts)

Short row 1 (back of head shaping): Sc2tog 4 times. Ch 1, turn.

Short row 2: Sc2tog twice. Ch 1, turn.

Round 21: Sc tbl in each st around (8 sts)

Fold one of the pipe cleaners into thirds and then twist together.

Insert into the nose through the head. The excess will extend inside the head. Stuff head.

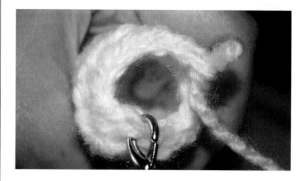

Rounds 22–23: Sc in next 4 sts, hdc in next 4 sts. (8 sts)

Round 24: Hdc in next 2 sts, sc in next 6 sts. (8 sts)

Round 25: Sc in each st around. (8 sts)

Round 26: Sc in next 3 sts, 2 sc in each of next 3 sts, sc in next 2 sts. (11 sts)

Round 27: Sc in next 3 sts, [sc in next st, 2 sc in next st] 3 times, sc in next 2 sts. (14 sts)

Round 28: Hdc in each st around. (14 sts)

Round 29: Hdc in next 5 sts, hdc2tog, hdc in next 2 sts, hdc2tog, hdc in next 3 sts. (12 sts)

Round 30: Hdc in next 3 sts, hdc2tog, hdc in next 4 sts, hdc2tog, hdc in next st. (10 sts)

Round 31: Hdc in next 3 sts, hdc2tog twice, hdc in next 3 sts. (8 sts)

Stuff neck lightly.

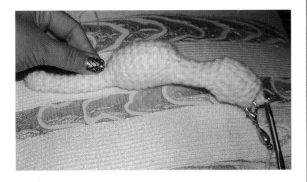

Round 32: Sc in each st around. (8 sts)

Round 33: Hdc in next 3 sts, 2 hdc in each of next 2 sts, hdc in next 3 sts. (10 sts)

Round 34: Hdc in next 4 sts, 2 hdc in each of next 2 sts, hdc in next 4 sts. (12 sts)

Round 35: Hdc in next 5 sts, 2 hdc in each of next 2 sts, hdc in next 5 sts. (14 sts)

Rounds 36–37: Hdc in each st around. (14 sts)

Round 38: Hdc in next 5 sts, hdc2tog twice, hdc in next 5 sts. (12 sts)

Rounds 39–40: Hdc in each st around. (12 sts)

Round 41: Hdc in next 4 sts, hdc2tog twice, hdc in next 4 sts. (10 sts)

Round 42: Hdc in each st around. (10 sts)

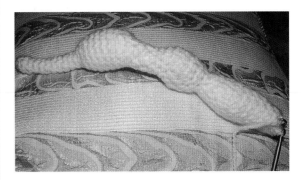

Stuff body.

Round 43: Hdc in next 3 sts, hdc2tog twice, hdc in next 3 sts. (8 sts)

Round 44: Hdc in next 2 sts, hdc2tog twice, hdc in next 2 sts. (6 sts)

Rounds 45–47: Hdc in each st around. (6 sts)

Stuff the end of the body a bit more.

Flatten the end of the tube and sc2tog across the end to hold it in place.

Ch 26.

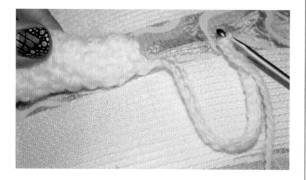

Tail row 1: Sc in 2nd ch from hook and in next 24 chs; sc in base of body. (26 sts)

Tail row 2: Ch 1, turn; sk sc in base of tail; sc in each st down length of tail. (25 sts)

Tail row 3: Ch 1, turn; sc in each st down length of tail to last st, sl st in last st. (25 sts)

Fasten off, leaving a long tail. Use the tail to sew the edges of the tail together with mattress stitch to form a long tube.

Thread a pipe cleaner into a yarn needle. Use the needle to thread the pipe cleaner through the tail, from the top to the base.

Cut off any excess pipe cleaner. Shape the tail as desired.

LEAF APPENDAGES

You can add as many leaf appendages as you like to your sea dragon; the length and placement of the appendages is also variable. Refer to the finished photos as a general guide.

Cut several 24-inch lengths of yarn (one for each appendage desired).

To add an appendage: Insert hook into sea dragon in any spot. Fold one of the cut lengths of yarn in half and use the hook to pull up a loop from the center of this piece. Using both strands of yarn, chain to the desired length. Fasten off and trim ends.

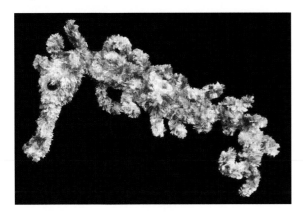

Here are the lengths used in the pictured sample:
Top of head: ch 5
Back of head: ch 7
Neck: ch 8
Chest: ch 10
Back: ch 10
Lower Back: ch 11
Belly: ch 7
Lower Belly: ch 5
Tail: ch 5

Cut several lengths of yarn 3 to 5 inches long (about three or four for each appendage). Take two pieces of yarn, fold in half, and pull up a loop from the center through one of the appendages. Pull the ends of the yarn through the loop and pull tight to secure.

Add loops on both sides of the appendage for a branched effect. Continue adding loops until you achieve the look you want.

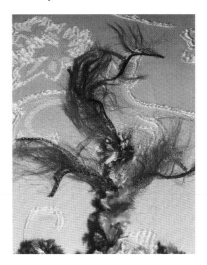

Variation

Make the crocheted appendages on the back of the sea dragon only. Add loops of varying lengths of yarn randomly across the body.

FINISHING
Clip the wire on the eyes so that it is around $1/2$ inch long. Test the fit of the eyes, referring to the photos for placement. Stitch through head where the eyes will go with a bit of yarn, pulling tightly to create a socket for the eyes to sit in. Tie off the yarn and bury the ends inside the head. Glue the eyes on with E-6000 in the center of the socket.

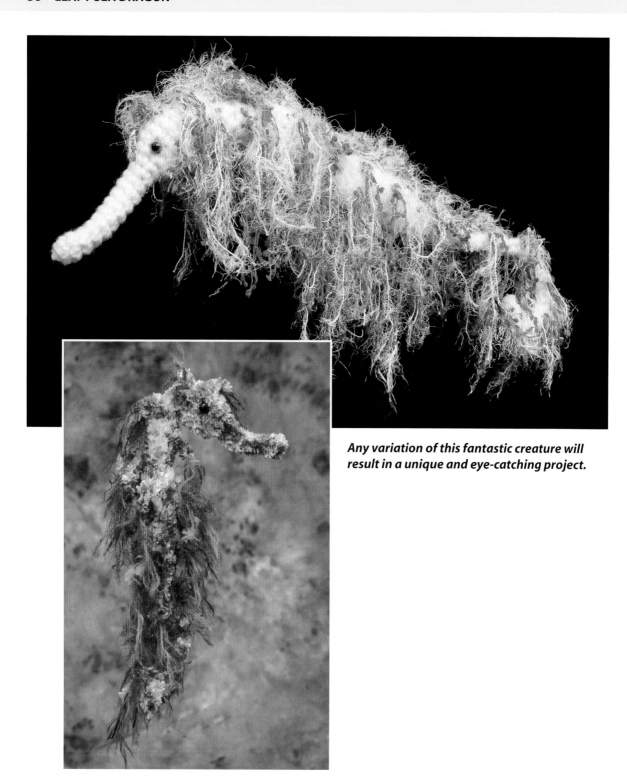

Any variation of this fantastic creature will result in a unique and eye-catching project.

Little Octopus

Designed by Vicky Lewis • (https://www.etsy.com/shop/thebirdsandbees)

This adorable little octopus doesn't seem to be having a great day—but his quirky expression is sure to make your day brighter! The features can be embroidered or needle-felted after the octopus is complete, so he is easy to customize. Since it doesn't need to end up any particular size, this is a great project for trying out felting for the first time.

4

Medium

YARN
Worsted-weight 100% wool yarn (not superwash) in green (20 yards) and gray (60 yards)
Scrap amounts of 100% wool yarn or roving (for needle felting) in black, dark gray, and white

HOOK
Size I-9 (5.5 mm) crochet hook

NOTIONS
Yarn needle
Polyester fiberfill
Liquid soap
Kitchen sink, washing machine, or dryer
Felting needles or embroidery needle

FINISHED MEASUREMENTS
3 inches tall; 7 inches wide

PATTERN

HEAD

With green, ch 2.

Round 1: 6 sc in 2nd ch from hook. (6 sts)

Round 2: Starting in first sc of round 1 to work in round, work 2 sc in each st. (12 sts)

Round 3: *Sc in next st, 2 sc in next st; rep from * around. (18 sts)

Round 4: *Sc in next 2 sts, 2 sc in next st; rep from * around. (24 sts)

Round 5: *Sc in next 3 sts, 2 sc in next st; rep from * around. (30 sts)

Round 6: *Sc in next 4 sts, 2 sc in next st; rep from * around. (36 sts)

Round 7–9: Sc in each st around. (36 sts)

Break off green and join gray.

Rounds 10–14: Sc in each st around. (36 sts)

Round 15: *Sc in next 4 sts, sk next st; rep from * around to last st, sc in last st. (29 sts)

Round 16: *Sc in next 3 sts, sk next st; rep from * around to last st, sc in last st. (22 sts)

Stuff lightly with fiberfill.

Round 17: *Sc in next 2 sts, sk next st; rep from * around. (15 sts)

Rep round 17 until opening is closed.

Fasten off and weave in ends.

ARMS (MAKE 8)

With gray, ch 2.

Round 1: 9 dc in 2nd ch from hook. (9 sts)

Round 2: Starting in first sc of round 1 to work in round, work sc in each st. (9 sts)

Rounds 3–11: Sc in each st around. (9 sts)

Fasten off, leaving a long tail to use to attach arm to body.

Stuff with gray yarn (unlike fiberfill, the yarn will felt, making it easier to felt and shape the arms).

HAT BRIM

Row 1: Join green to head on border between green and gray. Working around the sts of the head, pick up 10 sts along the edge of the green area, sl st in next st. Ch 1, turn. (11 sts)

Row 2: Sk sl st, hdc in next 10 sts. Ch 1, turn. (10 sts)

Row 3: Hdc in next 10 sts. Ch 1, turn. (10 sts)

Row 4: Sk first st, hdc in next 7 sts, sk 1 st, sl st in last st. Ch 1, turn. (8 sts)

Row 5: Sk sl st, hdc in next 7 sts, sl st in same st as last hdc.

Fasten off and weave in ends.

ASSEMBLY

Use tails left when fastening off to sew arms to the bottom of the head, spacing them out evenly on all sides. Weave in all ends.

FELTING

You can felt your octopus in a washing machine or in a sink.

FELTING WITH A WASHING MACHINE

Note

This method may not work as well with modern washers with the temperature capped at 120 degrees or even less.

With your washing machine at its lowest water setting, fill the machine with very hot tap water. Put your crocheted project in. Add dish detergent and let the washer go through the first wash cycle. Do not spin or rinse. Check your project after the first cycle to see if it's felted the way you want. If it needs more felting, let it go through another wash cycle. I usually put the project through two 12-minute agitations; some yarns require more. When you are satisfied the work is felted, rinse it with cold water and squeeze out as much water as possible. Shape your project to the look you want, then let it dry completely.

FELTING IN THE KITCHEN SINK

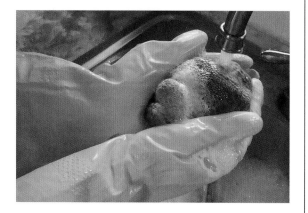

You can also felt this or any other project in your kitchen sink. Wear heavy rubber gloves to protect your hands from the heat. Run your sink half full of very hot water (as hot as you can stand) and put your crocheted project in with a small amount of liquid soap on it. Dunk the project in and out of the hot water, rubbing it to felt the fibers. Do this for a minute and then run it under very cold water, still rubbing it the whole time. Repeat the hot and cold treatment until the project has shrunk slightly and felted (about 4 or 5 cycles). When you are satisfied with the felting of the work, give it a final rinse under cold water, and then squeeze out as much water as possible. Shape your project to the look you want. Let it dry completely.

FINISHING

Embroider the octopus's facial features with a yarn needle and scrap amounts of yarn, or needle-felt the features with yarn or roving. If you want, you can needle-felt a piece of green yarn around the bottom edge of the hat for a clean line between hat and head.

He's lonely—make him some friends!

Horseshoe Crab

Designed by Susan K. Burkhart • (http://www.OohLookItsARabbit.etsy.com)

People who've spent vacations on the Chesapeake Bay or the Atlantic Ocean, like the designer of this project, will remember seeing many of these crabs along the beach. Horseshoe crabs actually are more closely related to spiders and scorpions than crabs. Fossils of these creatures have been found that date back 450 million years. You'll learn a little arthropod anatomy as you crochet this intricately constructed project!

YARN
Worsted-weight yarn in brown (approximately 8 oz)

HOOK
Size F-5 (3.75 mm) crochet hook

NOTIONS
Two 10 or 12 mm black safety eyes (or substitute embroidery for a toy for small children)
Polyester fiberfill
Pipe cleaners for alternate version of legs

FINISHED MEASUREMENTS
17 inches long

PATTERN

BOTTOM CARAPACE PLATE

Ch 2.

Row 1: Sc in second ch from hook, ch 1 and turn. (1 sc)

Row 2: 2 sc in next st, ch 1 and turn. (2 sc)

Row 3: Sc in next st, 2 sc in next st, ch 1 and turn. (3 sc)

Row 4: 2 sc in next st, sc in next 2 sts, ch 1 and turn. (4 sc)

Row 5: 2 sc in next st, sc in next 2 sts, 2 sc in next st, ch 1 and turn. (6 sc)

Row 6: 2 sc in next st, sc in next 5 sts, ch 1 and turn. (7 sc)

Row 7: Sc in next 6 sts, 2 sc in next st, ch 1 and turn. (8 sc)

Row 8: 2 sc in next st, sc in next 7 sts, ch 1 and turn. (9 sc)

Row 9: Sc in next 8 sts, 2 sc in next st, ch 25 and turn. (10 sc + 25 chs)

Row 10: 2 sc in in 2nd ch from hook, sc in next 23 ch, sc in next 9 sts, 2 sc in next st, ch 1 and turn. (36 sc)

Row 11–13: Sc in each st across, ch 1 and turn. (36 sc)

Row 14: 2 sc in next st, sc in next 34 sts, 2 sc in next st, ch 1 and turn. (38 sc)

Row 15–17: Sc in each st across, ch 1 and turn. (38 sc)

Row 18: Sc2tog, sc in next 34 sts, sc2tog, ch 1 and turn. (36 sc)

Row 19–21: Sc in each st across, ch 1 and turn. (36 sc)

Row 22: Sc2tog, sc in next 32 sts, sc2tog, ch 1 and turn. (34 sc)

Row 23–25: Sc in each st across, ch 1 and turn. (34 sc)

Row 26: Sc2tog, sc in next 30 sts, sc2tog, ch 1 and turn. (32 sc)

Row 27–28: Sc in each st across, ch 1 and turn. (32 sc)

Row 29: Sc2tog, sc in next 28 sts, sc2tog, ch 1 and turn. (30 sc)

Row 30: Sc in each st across, ch 1 and turn. (30 sc)

Row 31: Sc2tog, sc in next 26 sts, sc2tog, ch 1 and turn. (28 sc)

Row 32: Sc2tog, sc in next 24 sts, sc2tog, ch 1 and turn. (26 sc)

Row 33: Sc2tog, sc in next 22 sts, sc2tog, ch 1 and turn. (24 sc)

Row 34: Sc2tog, sc in next 20 sts, sc2tog, ch 1 and turn. (22 sc)

Row 35: Sc2tog, sc in next 18 sc, sc2tog, ch 1 and turn. (20 sc)

Row 36: Sc2tog 2 times, sc in next 12 sts, sc2tog 2 times, ch 1 and turn. (16 sc)

Row 37: Sc2tog 2 times, sc in next 8 sts, sc2tog 2 times, ch 1 and turn. (12 sc)

Row 38: Sc2tog 2 times, sc in next 4 sts, sc2tog 2 times. (8 sc)

Fasten off, leaving enough yarn to sew at least halfway around this plate.

Rejoin main yarn in the 11th stitch from the end of row 9 in the unused loops of the chain to make the second point.

Row 1: Sc2tog, sc in next 8 sts, ch 1 and turn. (9 sts)

Row 2: Sc in next 7 sts, sc2tog, ch 1 and turn. (8 sts)

Row 3: Sc2tog, sc in next 6 sts, ch 1 and turn. (7 sts)

Row 4: Sc in next 5 sts, sc2tog, ch 1 and turn. (6 sts)

Row 5: Sc2tog, sc in next 2 sts, sc2tog, ch 1 and turn. (4 sts)

Row 6: Sc in next 2 sts, sc2tog, ch 1 and turn. (3 sts)

Row 7: Sc2tog, sc in next st, ch 1 and turn. (2 sts)

Row 8: Sc2tog. (1 sts)

Fasten off, leaving enough yarn to sew at least halfway around plate. Weave in all ends except the two long pieces.

FLANGE OR PROSOMA (HEAD)

Ch 2.

Round 1: 6 sc in 2nd ch from hook (OR create magic ring and make 6 sc in ring). (6 sc)

Round 2: Working in a continuous spiral, 2 sc in 1st sc of round 1, 2 sc in each of next 5 sts. (12 sc)

Round 3: *2 sc in next st, sc in next st; rep from * around. (18 sc)

Round 4: *Sc in next 2 sts, 2 sc in next st; rep from * around. (24 sc)

Round 5: *2 sc in next st, sc in next 3 sts; rep from * around. (30 sc)

Round 6: Sc in next 2 sts, [2 sc in next st, sc in next 4 sts] 5 times, 2 sc in next st, sc in next 2 sts. (36 sc)

Round 7: *2 sc in next st, sc in next 5 sts; rep from * around. (42 sc)

Round 8: Sc in next 3 sts, [2 sc in next st, sc in next 6 sts] 5 times, 2 sc in next st, sc in next 3 sts. (48 sc)

Round 9: *2 sc in next st, sc in next 7 sts; rep from * around. (54 sc)

Round 10: Sc in next 4 sts, [2 sc in next st, sc in next 8 sts] 5 times, 2 sc in next st, sc in next 4 sts. (60 sc)

Round 11: *2 sc in next st, sc in next 14 sts; rep from * around. (64 sc)

Round 12: Sc in next 7 sts, [2 sc in next st, sc in next 15 sts] 3 times, 2 sc in next st, sc in next 8 sts. (68 sc)

Round 13: Sc in next 3 sts, [2 sc in next st, sc in next 16 sts] 3 times, 2 sc in next st, sc in next 13 sts. (72 sc)

Round 14: Sc in each st around. (72 sc)

Round 15: *2 sc in next st, sc in next 17 sts; rep from * around. (76 sc)

Round 16: Sc in each st around. (76 sc)

Round 17: Sc in next 8 sts, [2 sc in next st, sc in next 18 sts] 3 times, 2 sc in next st, sc in next 10 sts. (80 sc)

Round 18: Sc in each st around. (80 sc)

Round 19: Sc in next 4 sts, [2 sc in next st, sc in next 19 sts] 3 times, 2 sc in next st, sc in next 15 sts. (84 sc)

Round 20: *2 sc in next st, sc in next 20 sts; rep from * around. (88 sc)

Round 21: Sc in next 10 sts, [2 sc in next st, sc in next 21 sts] 3 times, 2 sc in next st, sc in next 11 sts. (92 sc)

Round 22: Sc in next 14 sts, [2 sc in next st, sc in next 22 sts] 3 times, 2 sc in next st, sc in next 8 sts. (96 sc)

Round 23: Sc in next 18 sts, [2 sc in next st, sc in next 23 sts] 3 times, 2 sc in next st, sc in next 5 sts. (100 sc)

Round 24: *2 sc in next st, sc in next 24 sts; rep from * around. (104 sc)

Round 25: *2 sc in next st, sc in next 12 sts; rep from * around. (112 sc)

Round 26: Sc in next 3 sts, [2 sc in next st, sc in next 13 sts] 7 times, 2 sc in next st, sc in next 10 sts. (120 sc)

Round 27: Sc in next 9 sts, [2 sc in next st, sc in next 14 sts] 7 times, 2 sc in next st, sc in next 5 sts. (128 sc)

Round 28–31: Sc in each st around. (128 sc)

Fasten off. If you are using safety eyes, insert them now. Mine were inserted about 13 rows from the bottom and about 26 stitches apart.

EYEBROWS (MAKE 2)

Ch 9.

Row 1: Sc in 2nd ch from hook, sc in next st, 2 sc in each of next 4 sts, sc in next 2 sts. (12 sc)

Fasten off, leaving enough yarn to sew eyebrow onto head. Sew onto head above eye, slightly covering the top of the eye. Weave in any remaining pieces of yarn.

BODY ASSEMBLY

Push in the back side of the dome to shape as shown in the picture, making sure the eyes are on the sides and slightly toward the front.

Carefully pin bottom carapace plate about 4 to 5 rows in from the bottom of the prosoma dome. Sew and stuff. Do not overstuff, as this will puff out the bottom carapace plate too much, leaving no room for the legs. I found it easiest to sew the points first, working around both sides toward the front, and stuffing from an opening in the front before sewing that opening closed.

OPISTHOSOMA (ABDOMEN)

For this piece, you will be working an oval rather than a circle. You will begin as if you were crocheting a row. When you reach the end of the beginning chain, rotate your work 180 degrees and continue in the unused loops on the other side of the foundation chain.

Ch 17.

Round 1: 2 sc in 2nd ch from hook, sc in next 14 sts, 3 sc in last ch, continue on other side of foundation chain and work 15 sc in the unused loops on the back of the ch. (34 sc)

Round 2: *Sc in next st, 2 sc in next st, sc in next 14 sts, 2 sc in next st; rep from * around. (38 sc)

Round 3: *Sc in next 2 sts, 2 sc in next st, sc in next 15 sts, 2 sc in next st; rep from * around. (42 sc)

Round 4: Sc tbl in each st around. (42 sc)

Round 5: [Sc in next 7 sts, 2 sc in next st] 2 times, sc in next 26 sts. (44 sc)

Round 6: Sc in next 8 sts, 2 sc in next st, sc in next 7 sts, 2 sc in next st, sc in next 27 sts. (46 sc)

Round 7: [Sc in next 6 sts, 2 sc in next st] 3 times, sc in next 25 sts. (49 sc)

Round 8: Sc in next 4 sts, 2 sc in next st, [sc in next 10 sts, 2 sc in next st] 2 times, sc in next 22 sts. (52 sc)

Round 9–15: Sc in each st around. (52 sc)

Round 16: Sc in next 20 sts, 2 sc in next st, sc in next 31 sts. (53 sc)

Round 17: Sc in each st around. (53 sc)

Fasten off, leaving enough yarn to sew abdomen onto head. Stuff abdomen and sew the open end onto the head between the two points. Notice that this piece has a flat side and an upwardly sloping side. The flat side is the bottom.

LARGE BACK POINTS (MAKE 2)

Ch 2.

Round 1: 4 sc in 2nd ch from hook (OR create magic ring and make 4 sc in ring). (4 sc)

Round 2: Continuing in a spiral in the 1st stitch of round 1, *2 sc in next st, sc in next st; rep from * around. (6 sc)

Round 3: *Sc in next st, 2 sc in next st, sc in next st; rep from * around. (8 sc)

Round 4: * 2 sc in next st, sc in next 3 sts; rep from * around. (10 sc)

Round 5: *Sc in next 2 sc, 2 sc in next st, sc in next 2 sts; rep from * around. (12 sc)

Round 6: * 2 sc in next st, sc in next 5 sts; rep from * around. (14 sc)

Round 7: Sc in next 3 sts, 2 sc in next st, sc in next 6 sts, 2 sc in next st, sc in next 3 sts. (16 sc)

Round 8: *2 sc in next st, sc in next 7 sts; rep from * around. (18 sc)

Round 9: Sc in next 3 sts, 2 sc in next st, sc in next 8 sts, 2 sc in next st, sc in next 5 sts. (20 sc)

Fasten off, leaving enough yarn to sew onto abdomen. These pieces will be attached later, after you crochet the tail spine.

TELSON (TAIL SPINE)

Ch 2.

Round 1: 4 sc in 2nd ch from hook (OR create magic ring and make 4 sc in ring). (4 sc)

Round 2: Continuing in a spiral in the 1st stitch of round 1, sc in each st around. (4 sc)

Rounds 3–4: Sc in each st around. (4 sc)

Round 5: 2 sc in next st, sc in next 3 sts. (5 sc)

Round 6–7: Sc in each st around. (5 sc)

Round 8: 2 sc in next st, sc in next 4 sts. (6 sc)

Round 9–10: Sc in each st around. (6 sc)

Round 11: 2 sc in next st, sc in next 5 sts. (7 sc)

Round 12–13: Sc in each st around. (7 sc)

Round 14: 2 sc in next st, sc in next 6 sts. (8 sc)

Round 15–16: Sc in each st around. (8 sc)

Round 17: 2 sc in next st, sc in next 7 sts. (9 sc)

Round 18–19: Sc in each st around. (9 sc)

Round 20: 2 sc in next st, sc in next 8 sts. (10 sc)

Round 21–22: Sc in each st around. (10 sc)

Round 23: 2 sc in next st, sc in next 9 sts. (11 sc)

Round 24–25: Sc in each st around. (11 sc)

Round 26: 2 sc in next st, sc in next 10 sts. (12 sc)

Round 27–28: Sc in each st around. (12 sc)

Round 29: 2 sc in next st, sc in next 11 sts. (13 sc)

Round 30–31: Sc in each st around. (13 sc)

Round 32: 2 sc in next st, sc in next 12 sts. (14 sc)

Round 33–34: Sc in each st around. (14 sc)

Round 35: 2 sc in next st, sc in next 13 sts. (15 sc)

Round 36–37: Sc in each st around. (15 sc)

Round 38: 2 sc in next st, sc in next 14 sts. (16 sc)

Round 39–40: Sc in each st around. (16 sc)

Round 41: 2 sc in next st, sc in next 15 sts. (17 sc)

Round 42–43: Sc in each st around. (17 sc)

Round 44: 2 sc in next st, sc in next 16 sts. (18 sc)

Round 45–46: Sc in each st around. (18 sc)

Round 47: 2 sc in next st, sc in next 17 sts. (19 sc)

Round 48–49: Sc in each st around. (19 sc)

Round 50: 2 sc in next st, sc in next 18 sts. (20 sc)

Round 51–52: Sc in each st around. (20 sc)

Fasten off, leaving enough yarn to sew tail spine onto abdomen. Stuff firmly.

Sew the abdomen points and tail spine onto the abdomen, on the round where you crocheted in the back loops only, with the tail spine in the middle and the points on either side. The easiest way to do this is to start with the side points. Sew most of the way around, leaving about 5 sc unattached (the 5 sc running top to bottom that will be touching the tail spine). At this point, there should be 5 sc on the top of the abdomen and 5 sc on the bottom of the abdomen that were not used to sew on the points. There should also be 5 sc on each point. Sew the tail spine to these remaining stitches.

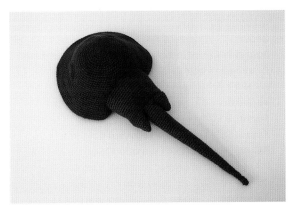

SMALL ABDOMEN SPINES (MAKE 6)

Ch 6.

Row 1: Sc in 2nd ch from hook, sc in next 4 sts, ch 1 and turn. (5 sc)

Row 2: Sc2tog, sc in next 3 sts, ch 1 and turn. (4 sc)

Row 3: Sc2tog, sc in next 2 sts, ch 1 and turn. (3 sc)

Row 4: Sc2tog, sc in next st, ch 1 and turn. (2 sc)

Row 5: Sc2tog. (1 sc)

Fasten off, leaving a length of yarn for sewing. Fold the triangle in half and sew the edges together. Add a little stuffing if you like. Use the remaining yarn to sew

the piece onto the side of the abdomen at the bottom edge. Sew three small spines onto each side of the abdomen. Weave in any remaining pieces of yarn.

LEGS (MAKE 5)

> ### Note
>
> Stuff the legs as you crochet them. Because they are so narrow, you will need to add stuffing every couple of rows.

Ch 2.

Round 1: 4 sc in 2nd ch from hook (OR create magic ring and make 4 sc in ring). (4 sc)

Round 2–3: Sc in each st around. (4 sc)

Round 4: 2 sc in next st, sc in next 3 sts. (5 sc)

Round 5: Sc in each st around. (5 sc)

Round 6: 2 sc in each of next 2 sts, sc in next st, sc2tog. (6 sc)

Round 7: 2 sc in each of next 2 sts, sc2tog 2 times. (6 sc)

Round 8: Sc2tog, 2 sc in each of next 2 sts, sc2tog. (6 sc)

Round 9: Sc in next 3 sts, 2 sc in next st, sc in next 2 sts. (7 sc)

Round 10–11: Sc in each st around. (7 sc)

Round 12: Sc2tog 2 times, 2 sc in each of next 2 sts, sc in next st. (7 sc)

Round 13: Sc2tog 2 times, 2 sc in each of next 2 sts, sc in next st. (7 sc)

Round 14: 2 sc in next st, sc2tog 2 times, sc in next st, 2 sc in next st. (7 sc)

Round 15: Sc in each st around. (7 sc)

Round 16: 2 sc in next st, sc2tog 2 times, sc in next st, 2 sc in next st. (7 sc)

Round 17: 2 sc in next st, sc in next st, sc2tog 2 times, 2 sc in next st. (7 sc)

Round 18: 2 sc in each of next 2 sts, sc in next st, sc2tog 2 times. (7 sc)

Round 19: Sc in each st around. (7 sc)

Round 20: 2 sc in next st, sc2tog 2 times, sc in next st, 2 sc in next st. (7 sc)

Round 21: Sc2tog 2 times, sc in next st, 2 sc in each of next 2 sts. (7 sc)

Round 22–26: Sc in each st around. (7 sc)

Round 27: 2 sc in next st, sc2tog 2 times, sc in next st, 2 sc in next st. (7 sc)

Round 28: 2 sc in next st, sc in next st, sc2tog 2 times, 2 sc in next st. (7 sc)

Round 29: Sc in each st around. (7 sc)

Round 30: 2 sc in each of next 2 sts, sc in next st, sc2tog 2 times. (7 sc)

Round 31: Sc2tog, 2 sc in each of next 2 sts, sc in next st, sc2tog. (7 sc)

Round 32: Sc2tog, 2 sc in each of next 2 sts, sc in next st, sc2tog. (7 sc)

Round 33: Sc in each st around. (7 sc)

Round 34: 2 sc in next st, sc in next st, 2 sc in next st, sc2tog 2 times. (7 sc)

Round 35: 2 sc in next st, sc in next st, 2 sc in next st, sc2tog 2 times. (7 sc)

Round 36: Sc2tog, 2 sc in each of next 2 sts, sc in next st, sc2tog. (7 sc)

Round 37–38: Sc in each st around. (7 sc)

Round 39: Sc in next 5 sts, sc2tog. (6 sc)

Round 40: Sc2tog 2 times, 2 sc in each of next 2 sts. (6 sc)

Round 41: Sc2tog 2 times, 2 sc in each of next 2 sts. (6 sc)

Round 42: Sc2tog 2 times, 2 sc in next st, sc in next st. (5 sc)

Round 43: Sc in each st around. (5 sc)

Round 44: Sc in next st, sc2tog, sc in next 2 sts. (4 sc)

Round 45–46: Sc in each st around. (4 sc)

Fasten off and sew opening closed. There will be some gaps where the stuffing shows. Weave in scraps of brown yarn to cover them if you like.

ALTERNATE VERSION OF LEGS

Working the many decreases and increases of the legs is pretty difficult. Some crocheters suggested an alternative, which I am including here. This version has pipe cleaners instead of stuffing inside the legs to help them hold their shape.

Ch 2.

Round 1: 4 sc in 2nd ch from hook (OR create magic ring and make 4 sc in ring). (4 sc)

Round 2–3: Sc in each st around. (4 sc)

Round 4: 2 sc in next st, sc in next 3 sts. (5 sc)

Round 5: Sc in each st around. (5 sc)

Round 6: 2 sc in next st, sc in next 4 sts. (6 sc)

Round 7–8: Sc in each st around. (6 sc)

Round 9: 2 sc in next st, sc in next 5 sts. (7 sc)

Round 10–42: Sc in each st around. (7 sc)

Round 43: Sc in next 5 sts, sc2tog. (6 sc)

Round 44–45: Sc in each st around. (6 sc)

Twist two or three brown pipe cleaners together. Stuff into the leg, pushing as far down into the leg as possible. It helps to have the sharp ends of the wires folded over so they don't catch on the yarn.

Round 46: Sc in next 3 sc, sc2tog, sc in next st. (5 sc)

Round 47: Sc in each st around. (5 sc)

Cut off excess pipe cleaners and fold over the sharp ends.

Round 48: Sc in next 3 sc, sc2tog. (4 sc)

Round 49–50: Sc in each st around. (4 sc)

Fasten off. Sew end closed. Bend leg into shape.

FINISHING

Sew the five legs together along the straight middle section, then sew the whole thing to the bottom of the head section, leaving the ends of the legs to dangle freely. Weave in any remaining yarn ends.

The underside of this crawly creature is creepily realistic.

INSECTS

Dragonfly

Designed by Liz Ward • (http://http://www.etsy.com/shop/AmigurumiBarmy)

Crochet this lovely little dragonfly in blue, as shown here, or in green, orange, pink, or even stripes—there is a species out there in nature to match almost any color you could choose. Metallic thread held together with regular white yarn mimics the iridescence of the wings.

3 Light

YARN
DK-weight yarn in turquoise, navy, and white

HOOK
Size E-4 (3.5 mm) crochet hook

NOTIONS
Teal metallic thread
6 mm black toy eyes
Yarn needle
Polyester fiberfill
Scrap of felt
Sequins and seed beads
Sewing thread or fabric glue

FINISHED MEASUREMENTS
6^{1}/$_{2}$ inches long

PATTERN

BODY

Make a magic ring (OR ch 4 and sl st in beg ch to form ring).

Round 1: 6 sc in ring (6 sts)

Round 2: 2 sc in each st around. (12 sts)

Round 3: *2 sc in next st, sc in next st; rep from * around. (18 sts)

Round 4: *2 sc in next st, sc in next 2 sts; rep from * around. (24 sts)

Round 5: *2 sc in next st, sc in next 3 sts; rep from * around. (30 sts)

Round 6: Sc in each st around. (30 sts) Use a second piece of scrap yarn to mark this round (to refer to later when placing the eyes).

Rounds 7–8: Repeat round 6.

Round 9: *Sc2tog, sc in next 3 sts; rep from * around. (24 sts)

Round 10: *Sc2tog, sc in next 2 sts; rep from * around. (18 sts)

Round 11: *Sc in next st, sc2tog; rep from * around. (12 sts)

Place the eyes in round 6 (the one you marked), 11 stitches apart. Stuff the dragonfly's head.

Round 12: Sc in each st around. (12 sts)

Rounds 13–35: Repeat round 12, stuffing the body every few rounds as you go.

Round 36: *Sc in next st, 2 sc in next st; rep from * around. (18 sts)

Round 37: *2 sc in next st, sc in next st; rep from * around. (24 sts)

Round 38: Sc in each st around. (24 sts)

Round 39: *Sc2tog, sc in next 2 sts; rep from * around. (18 sts)

Round 40: *Sc in next st, sc2tog; rep from * around. (12 sts) Finish stuffing the body now.

Round 41: Sc2tog around. (6 sts)

Fasten off, leaving a long tail. Using a yarn needle, weave the tail through the last 6 sts and pull tight to close. Weave in ends and cut remaining yarn.

STRIPES

Cut a long length of navy yarn and, using a yarn needle, attach it to the body of the dragonfly, under the neck.

Wrap the yarn around the neck 3 times, pulling it tight. Fasten off.

Skip the next 7 rows and wrap the yarn around the next row in the same way as before.

Skip the next 4 rows and wrap the yarn around the next row, as before.

Skip 4 more rows and wrap the yarn around the next row.

Skip another 4 more rows and add the final 3 wraps of yarn around the next row.

Weave in ends.

WINGS

The wings are worked along the front and back of a chain so the foundation chain becomes the center of the wing.

Hold the white yarn and metallic thread together throughout to create glittery wings.

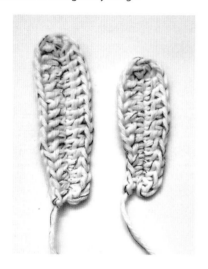

FRONT WINGS (MAKE 2)

Ch 17. Sc in 2nd ch from hook, sc in next ch, hdc in next 3 chs, dc in next 10 chs, 3 dc in last ch. Now turn and work along the back of the chain: 10 dc, 3 hdc, 2 sc. Fasten off.

BACK WINGS (MAKE 2)

Ch 13. Sc in 2nd ch from hook, sc in next ch, hdc in next 3 chs, dc in next 10 chs, 3 dc in last ch. Now turn and work along the back of the chain as follows: 5 dc, 3 hdc, 2 sc. Fasten off.

FINISHING

Sew the wings to the body of the dragonfly between the first 2 stripes. Weave in any remaining ends.

Cut a little flower out of blue felt. Decorate the center with sequins and seed beads and sew or glue it to the dragonfly's head.

Flower template

Aphid

Designed by Lisa Olivia Vanvikaas • (http://www.etsy.com/shop/hepp)

Aphids may be small (ranging from only 0.04 to 0.39 inch long), but they are a serious plant pest—one more reason why we love ladybugs, one of their natural predators, so much. But beware the ladybug who could eat this aphid—at 10 inches long, it is 100 times life size!

5 Bulky

YARN
Bulky-weight 100% wool yarn in light green and dark green, plus small amounts of red, black, and white

HOOKS
G-6 (4 mm) crochet hook
7 (4.5 mm) crochet hook

NOTIONS
Polyester fiberfill
Yarn needle

FINISHED MEASUREMENTS
10 inches long

PATTERN

HEAD AND BODY

With light green yarn and size 7 hook, make a magic ring.

Round 1: 6 sc in ring. (6 sts)

Round 2: 2 sc in each st around. (12 sts)

Round 3: *Sc in next st, 2 sc in next st; rep from * around. (18 sts)

Round 4: Sc in each st around. (18 sts)

Round 5: *Sc in next 2 sts, 2 sc in next st; rep from * around. (24 sts)

Round 6: *Sc in next 3 sts, 2 sc in next st; rep from * around. (30 sts)

Round 7: *Sc in next 4 sts, 2 sc in next st; rep from * around. (36 sts)

Round 8: *Sc in next 5 sts, 2 sc in next st; rep from * around. (42 sts)

Rounds 9–10: Sc in each st around. (42 sts)

Round 11: *Sc in next 5 sts, sc2tog; rep from * around. (36 sts)

Round 12: Sc in each st around. (36 sts)

Round 13: *Sc in next 4 sts, sc2tog; rep from * around. (30 sts)

Round 14: Sc in each st around. (30 sts)

Round 15: Fpsc in each st around. (30 sts)

Rounds 16–17: Sc in each st around. (30 sts)

Round 18: *Sc in next 4 sts, 2 sc in next st; rep from * around. (36 sts)

Round 19: Sc in each st around. (36 sts)

Round 20: *Sc in next 5 sts, 2 sc in next st; rep from * around. (42 sts)

Rounds 21–23: Sc in each st around. (42 sts)

Round 24: Fpsc in each st around. (42 sts)

Rounds 25–28: Sc in each st around. (42 sts)

Round 29: *Sc in next 13 sts, 2 sc in next st; rep from * around. (45 sts)

Rounds 30–31: Sc in each st around.

Round 32: *Sc in next 14 sts, 2 sc in next st; rep from * around. (48 sts)

Rounds 33–37: Sc in each st around. (48 sts)

Round 38: *Sc in next 14 sts, sc2tog; rep from * around. (45 sts)

Round 39: Sc in each st around. (45 sts)

Round 40: *Sc in next 13 sts, sc2tog; rep from * around. (42 sts)

Round 41: Sc in each st around. (42 sts)

Round 42: *Sc in next 12 sts, sc2tog; rep from * around. (39 sts)

Round 43: *Sc in next 11 sts, sc2tog; rep from * around. (36 sts)

Round 44: *Sc in next 4 sts, sc2tog; rep from * around. (30 sts)

Round 45: Sc in each st around. (30 sts)

Round 46: *Sc in next 3 sts, sc2tog; rep from * around. (24 sts)

Round 47: Sc in each st around.

Round 48: *Sc in next 2 sts, sc2tog; rep from * around. (18 sts)

Round 49: *Sc in next st, sc2tog; rep from * around. (12 sts)

Round 50: Sc in each st around. (12 sts)

Round 51: *Sc in next st, sc2tog; rep from * around. (8 sts)

Fasten off; weave the tail through the front loops of the last 8 sts and pull tight to close the hole. Weave in the end.

TAIL

With light green yarn and size 7 hook, make a magic ring.

Round 1: 5 sc in ring. (5 sts)

Round 2: 2 sc in next st, sc in next 4 sts. (6 sts)

Round 3: *Sc in next st, 2 sc in next st; rep from * around. (9 sts)

Round 4: Sc in each st around. (9 sts)

Round 5: *Sc in next 2 sts, 2 sc in next st; rep from * around. (12 sts)

Sl st in next st to even out round. Fasten off, leaving a long tail of yarn for assembly.

CORNICLES (MAKE 2)

With dark green yarn and size 7 hook, make a magic ring.

Round 1: 6 sc in ring. (6 sts)

Rounds 2–9: Sc in each st around. (6 sts)

Round 10: *Sc in next st, 2 sc in next st; rep from * around. (9 sts)

Sl st in next st to even out round. Fasten off, leaving a long tail.

LEGS (MAKE 6)

With dark green yarn and size 7 hook, make a magic ring.

Round 1: 6 sc in ring. (6 sts)

Round 2: 2 sc in each st around. (12 sts)

Round 3: *Sc in next 2 sts, 2 sc in next st; rep from * around. (16 sts)

Rounds 4–6: Sc in each st around. (16 sts)

Round 7: *Sc in next 2 sts, sc2tog; rep from * around. (12 sts)

Stuff foot.

Round 8: Sc2tog around. (6 sts)

Round 9: Sc2tog around. (3 sts)

Ch 14; sc in 2nd ch from hook, sl st in next ch and in each ch to end. Sl st in top of foot (round 9). Fasten off.

EYES (MAKE 2)

With black yarn and size G–6 hook, make a magic ring.

Round 1: 6 sc in ring. (6 sts)

Change to red yarn.

Round 2: Work 2 sc in each st around. (12 sts)

Change to white yarn.

Rounds 3–4: Sc in each st around. (12 sts)

Sl st in next st to even out round; fasten off, leaving a long tail.

EYELIDS (MAKE 2)

With light green yarn and size 7 hook, ch 9.

Row 1: Sc in 2nd ch from hook, hdc in next ch, 2 dc in next ch, dc in next 2 chs, 2 dc in next ch, hdc in next ch, 3 sc in last ch. Turn piece and work in the unused loops along the other side of the chain: Hdc in 2nd ch from hook and next 5 chs, sc in last ch, sl st in same ch. (20 sts)

Fasten off, leaving a long tail.

ANTENNA BASES (MAKE 2):

With light green yarn and size G-6 hook, make a magic ring.

Round 1: 6 sc in ring. (6 sts)

Round 2: *Sc in next st, 2 sc in next st; rep from * around. (9 sts)

Round 3-4: Sc in each st around. (9 sts)

Sl st in next st to even out round; fasten off, leaving a long tail.

ANTENNAE (MAKE 2)

With dark green yarn and size G–6 hook, make a magic ring.

Round 1: 6 sc in ring. (6 sts)

Rounds 2–36: Sc in each st around. (6 sts)

Sl st in next st to even out round; fasten off, leaving a long tail.

ASSEMBLING THE APHID

Sew the tail to the back end of the aphid with the long tail of light green yarn you left. The tip of the tail should be pointing slightly upwards.

The cornicles do not need to be stuffed. Use the long tails you left to sew them to the aphid's back, 13 rounds back from the fpsc round (round 24) and 7 sts apart. They should be pointing back and a little outwards.

Attach the legs to the sides of the aphid's thorax using dark green yarn. Try to space the legs out evenly in this narrow area.

Embroider the mouth with red yarn.

Sew the eyes to the sides of the head using white yarn. Don't worry if the color changes in the eyes look a little messy or uneven; turn the eye so the color changes are in the top half, and the eyelids will cover them.

Place the eyelids over the eyes, with the side with the dcs on the top. Sew in place along the top edge. Do not sew the eyelids to the eye itself; the edge of the hdc row should be free.

Stuff the antenna bases quite firmly so they will support the weight of the antennae. Attach them right above the front edge of the eyelids. Sew the antennae to the bases so that they point towards the back.

Look out, garden plants!

Butterfly

Designed by Greta Tulner • (http://www.ATERGcrochet.Etsy.com)

Butterflies just might be the prettiest of all insects. They come in all colors of the rainbow—and in some cultures, those colors have a traditional meaning. If the first butterfly of spring is white, the summer will be rainy; if it's yellow, it'll be sunny; and if it's dark, expect lots of thunderstorms. Ensure the kind of summer you want by making this butterfly in any color combination of your choice (a great way to use up scraps of brightly colored yarn). Display your creation on a tote bag or jacket.

1 Super Fine

YARN
Fingering-weight cotton yarn in 5 colors

HOOK
Size B-1 (2.5 mm) crochet hook

NOTIONS
Yarn needle

FINISHED MEASUREMENTS
4 inches wide; 4 inches tall

SPECIAL STITCHES

Double crochet cluster (dc-cluster): Yo, insert hook where indicated in pattern, yo and pull up a loop, yo and pull through 2 loops (2 loops rem on hook); *yo, insert hook in same place as before, yo and pull up a loop, yo and pull through 2 loops; rep from * 2 more times (5 loops on hook at end of last repeat); yo and pull through all 5 loops.

Picot: Ch 3, sl st in first ch.

PATTERN

BOTTOM WING (MAKE 2)

With color A, ch 6; join with sl st to form a ring.

Round 1: Ch 3 (counts as first dc), 13 dc in ring; join with sl st in 3rd ch of beg ch–3. (14 sts)

Fasten off A.

Round 2: Join color B between any 2 dc of row 1 (counts as first sc). Ch 1, sc in sp between next 2 dc and in each sp around; join with sl st in beg ch. (14 sts, not counting ch)

Fasten off B.

Round 3: Join color C between any 2 sc of round 3. Ch 1, [dc, ch 2, dc, hdc] in same sp as joining, ch 1; [sc in next sp, ch 1] 6 times; in next sp [hdc, dc, ch 6, dc-cluster in 3rd ch from hook, ch 4, sl st in same ch as dc-cluster, sl st in next 3 chs, dc in same sp as first hdc, hdc in same sp], ch 1; [sc in next sp, ch 1] 6 times; join with sl st in beg ch.

Fasten off C.

With color D, work a circle of sl sts on the surface of the wing, working around the dc of round 1.

TOP WING (MAKE 2)

Work rounds 1–2 of bottom wing.

Round 3: Join color C between any two sc of round 2. Ch 1, [dc, ch 2, dc, hdc] in same sp as joining, ch 1; [sc in next sp, ch 1] 3 times; hdc in next sp, ch 1, dc in next sp, ch 1, 3 dc in next sp, [tr, picot, tr] in next sp, 3 dc in next sp, ch 1, dc in next sp, ch 1, hdc in next sp, ch 1; [sc in next sp, ch 1] 3 times; join with sl st in beg ch.

Fasten off C.

With color D, work a circle of sl sts on the surface of the wing, working around the dc of round 1.

Sew each top wing to a bottom wing.

BODY

With color E, ch 20.

Round 1: Dc-cluster in 3rd ch from hook, ch 4, sl st in same ch as dc-cluster, sl st in next 17 chs, ch 2; working along the back of the foundation chain, sl st in unused loops of next 17 chs; join with sl st in same ch as dc-cluster.

Fasten off, leaving a long tail. Wrap the yarn tail twice around neck, then tie off and trim excess.

Sew the wings on either side of the body.

You can quickly make a whole flock!

Ladybug

Designed by Mevlinn Gusick • (http://www.mevvsan.com)

Humans have a funny relationship with ladybugs. While we smash many beetles on sight
or, at best, ignore them as long as they stay a few
feet away, we love these little red-and-black beetles! We have nursery rhymes and picture books
about them and even wear them on our clothes
and jewelry. Here is a crocheted version with two
wing variations—one with the wings folded up (and
made in a single piece), the other with two separate wings spread and ready to "fly away home."

YARN
Worsted-weight yarn in
black, red, and white

4 Medium

HOOK
Size C-2 (2.75 mm) crochet hook
Size D-3 (3.25 mm) crochet hook

NOTIONS
Yarn needle
Polyester fiberfill
6 mm safety eyes

FINISHED MEASUREMENTS
3^{1}/$_{2}$ inches long

GAUGE
Gauge is flexible for this project.

PATTERN

BODY

Use the size C hook for the entire body. Make a magic ring (OR ch 5 and join with a sl st to form a ring).

Round 1: Work 6 sc in ring. (6 sts) Mark the end of the round but do not join; continue in a spiral throughout body.

Round 2: 2 sc tbl in each st. (12 sts)

Round 3: *2 sc tbl in next st, sc tbl in next st; repeat from* around. (18 sts)

Round 4: *2 sc tbl in next st, sc tbl in next 2 sts; repeat from* around. (24 sts)

Round 5: Repeat round 4. (32 sts)

Round 6: *2 sc tbl in next st, sc tbl in next 3 sts; repeat from* around. (40 sts)

Round 7: Sc tfl around. (40)

Rounds 8 and 9: Sc tbl around. (40)

Round 10: *Sc2tog tbl, sc tbl in next 3 sts; repeat from* around. (32 sts)

Round 11: Sc tbl around. (32 sts)

Stuff body, adding more stuffing as needed as you work the final rounds.

Round 12: *Sc2tog tbl, sc tbl in next 2 sts; repeat from* around. (24 sts)

Round 13: Repeat round 12. (18 sts)

Round 14: *Sc2tog tbl, sc tbl in next st; repeat from* around. (12 sts)

Round 15: *Sc2tog tbl in each st around. Fasten off.

Before you stuff and close up the body, make sure you have the piece turned wrong-side-out, so that the ridges from crocheting through the back loops are on the inside of the piece.

EYES (MAKE 2)

Make a magic ring (OR ch 4 and join with a sl st to form a ring).

Round 1: With the size C hook, work 4 sc in ring. Fasten off.

Push the front of the safety eye through the center of the magic ring. With the eye in the ring, put the back of the eye on.

HEAD

Make a magic ring (OR ch 4 and join with a sl st to form a ring).

Round 1: With size C hook, work 5 sc in ring. (5 sts)

Round 2: Work 2 sc tbl in each st. (10 sts)

Round 3: *2 sc tbl in next st, sc tbl in next st; repeat from* around. (15 sts)

Round 4: Sc tbl in each st around. (15 sts)

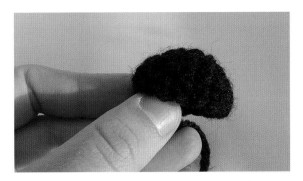

Fasten off. Attach the eyes, then stuff the head lightly and sew onto the body with the back side of the work to the outside.

OPEN WING (MAKE 2)

With size D hook, ch 4.

Row 1: 2 sc in second chain from hook, sc in next chain, 2 sc in next chain. Ch1, turn. (5 sts)

Row 2: 2 sc in first st, sc in each st to last st, 2 sc in last st. Ch1, turn. (7 sts)

Rows 3–6: Repeat row 2. (15 sts at end of row 6)

Row 7: Sc in each st across. (15 sts) Ch 1, do NOT turn.

Row 8: Sc around the entire edge of the wing. Fasten off.

Sew the front tips of the wings to the body (with the wrong side of the work facing up) and embroider spots on the wings with black yarn.

CLOSED WINGS

Use the size C hook for the entire body. Make a magic ring (or ch 5 and join with a sl st to form a ring).

Round 1: Work 6 sc in ring. (6 sts) Mark the end of the round but do not join; continue in a spiral throughout body.

Round 2: 2 sc tbl in each st. (12 sts)

Round 3: *2 sc tbl in next st, sc tbl in next st; repeat from* around. (18 sts)

Round 4: *2 sc tbl in next st, sc tbl in next 2 sts; repeat from* around. (24 sts)

Round 5: Repeat round 4. (32 sts)

Round 6: Sc tbl around. (32 sts)

Round 7: *2 sc tbl in next st, sc tbl in next 3 sts; repeat from* around. (40 sts)

Rounds 8 and 9: Sc tbl around. (40 sts)

Fasten off.

Embroider spots on the wings with black yarn, then sew the wings to the body with the wrong side of the work facing up.

LEGS

In the step-by-step photos, the legs have been worked in red to better show what is going on in each step. Normally they would be black.

With size C hook, sl st through the underside of the body where you want the first leg to be, just below the round of sc tfl (which will appear as a ridge on the surface of the work).

Ch 4, *sc twice in second ch from hook. Sl st in next 2 chs.**

Sl st through next 3 or 4 sts of underside of body until you reach the place where you want the next leg to be. Ch 4 and repeat from * to ** for the second leg.

Sl st through next 3 or 4 sts of underside of body and place another leg. Fasten off.

Repeat on opposite side of body.

Small in size but big on charm.

Mosquito

Designed by Stacey Trock • (http://www.freshstitches.com)

Normally, mosquitoes are pretty annoying . . . but not this one! He's too oversized to do too much buzzing around! This mosquito is a great first-time pattern—I often use him to teach folks new to amigurumi. The pattern uses only single crochet, and he only takes a couple of hours to complete.

YARN
Worsted-weight yarn in gray (40 yards) and white (20 yards)

4 Medium

HOOK
Size G-6 (4 mm) crochet hook

NOTIONS
Yarn needle
Polyester fiberfill
Two 12 mm black animal eyes

FINISHED MEASUREMENTS
7 inches long (including nose)

PATTERN

Note

Throughout this pattern, crochet through the back loop only.

LEGS (MAKE 4)

With gray, ch 2.

Round 1: Work 6 sc in 2nd ch from hook. (6 sts)

Round 2: Starting with the first st of round 1 to work in the round, sc in each st around. (6 sts)

Rounds 3–6: Sc in each st around.

Fasten off, leaving a long tail.

WINGS (MAKE 2)

With white, ch 2.

Round 1: Work 6 sc in 2nd ch from hook. (6 sts)

Round 2: Starting with the first st of round 1 to work in the round, work 2 sc in each st around. (12 sts)

Round 3: *2 sc in next st, sc in next st; repeat from * around. (18 sts)

Rounds 4–7: Sc in each st around. (18 sts)

Round 8: *Sc2tog, sc in next st; repeat from * around. (12 sts)

Fasten off, leaving a long tail.

BODY

With gray, ch 2.

Round 1: Work 6 sc in 2nd ch from hook. (6 sts)

Round 2: Starting with the first st of round 1 to work in the round, work 2 sc in each st around. (12 sts)

Round 3: *2 sc in next st, sc in next st; rep from * around. (18 sts)

Round 4: *2 sc in next st, sc in next 2 sts; rep from * around. (24 sts)

Round 5: *2 sc in next st, sc in next 3 sts; rep from * around. (30 sts)

Rounds 6–10: Sc in each st around. (30 sts)

Round 11: * Sc2tog, sc in next 3 sts; rep from * around. (24 sts)

Round 12: * Sc2tog, sc in next 2 sts; rep from * around. (18 sts)

Fasten off, leaving a long tail.

EYES (MAKE 2)

With white, ch 2.

Round 1: Work 6 sc in 2nd ch from hook. (6 sts)

Round 2: Starting with the first st of round 1 to work in the round, work 2 sc in each st around. (12 sts)

Round 3: *2 sc in next st, sc in next st; rep from * around. (18 sts)

Round 4: Sc in each st around. (18 sts)

Fasten off, leaving a long tail.

HEAD

With gray, ch 2.

Round 1: Work 6 sc in 2nd ch from hook. (6 sts)

Round 2: Starting with the first st of round 1 to work in the round, sc in each st around. (6 sts)

Rounds 3–11: Sc in each st around.

Round 12: Work 2 sc in each st around. (12 sts)

Round 13: *2 sc in next st, sc in next st; rep from * around. (18 sts)

Round 14: *2 sc in next st, sc in next 2 sts; rep from * around. (24 sts)

Round 15: *2 sc in next st, sc in next 3 sts; rep from * around. (30 sts)

Rounds 16–20: Sc in each st around. (30 sts)

Round 21: *Sc2tog, sc in next 3 sts; rep from * around. (24 sts)

Round 22: *Sc2tog, sc in next 2 sts; rep from * around. (18 sts)

Fasten off, leaving a long tail.

ASSEMBLY

Hold body so that opening is toward the side, as pictured. Flatten wings and attach to each side along round 10.

Attach legs evenly spaced along bottom of body.

Fasten the plastic eyes to the center of each crocheted eye by inserting the post of each eye between two stitches and pressing the washer onto the back post to secure the eye.

Stuff eyes and attach to the sides of the head (with the "nose" facing forward), as pictured.

Stuff head and body and sew together.

Weave in all ends.

If only all mosquitoes were this cute!

ARACHNIDS & MORE

Scorpion

Designed by Lisa Olivia Vanvikaas • (http://www.etsy.com/shop/hepp)

Scorpions carry their tails above their heads, ready to administer a painful or even deadly sting—but there's no need to fear this guy. Just look at that face! Be sure the hook and yarn you're using yield firm fabric, because you'll need to stuff this toy pretty tightly to get the tail to hold itself up.

5

Bulky

YARN
100% wool bulky-weight yarn in beige, light brown, dark brown, and yellow, plus small amounts of red, dark blue, black, and white

HOOKS
G-6 (4 mm) crochet hook
7 (4.5 mm) crochet hook

NOTIONS
Stuffing
Yarn needle

FINISHED MEASUREMENTS
12 inches long (not counting claws);
    8 inches tall

PATTERN

HEAD & BODY

With beige yarn and size 7 hook, make a magic ring.

Round 1: 6 sc in ring. (6 sts)

Round 2: 2 sc in each st around. (12 sts)

Round 3: *Sc in next st, 2 sc in next st; rep from * around. (18 sts)

Round 4: Sc in each st around. (18 sts)

Round 5: *Sc in next 3 sts, 2 sc in each of next 3 sts, sc in next 3 sts; rep from * around. (24 sts)

Round 6: Sc in each st around. (24 sts)

Round 7: *Sc in next 5 sts, 2 sc in each of next 3 sts, sc in next 4 sts; rep from * around. (30 sts)

Round 8: Sc in each st around. (30 sts)

Place marker in 2nd and 5th sts in next round – these mark the sides of the body

Round 9: *Sc in next 7 sts, 2 sc in each of next 2 sts, place marker in st just made, 2 sc in next st, sc in next 5 sts; rep from * around. (36 sts)

Round 10–17: Sc in each st around. (36 sts)

Round 18: *Sc in next 10 sts, 2 sc in each of next 3 sts, sc in next 5 sts; rep from * around. (42 sts)

Rounds 19–22: Sc in each st around. (42 sts)

Sc in next 4 sts (to the center of the bottom of the body). Place marker; this is the new starting point of every round. Change to brown yarn

Round 23: Bpsc in each st around. (42 sts)

Round 24: *Sc in next 9 sts, 2 sc in each of next 3 sts, sc in next 9 sts; rep from * around. (48 sts)

Rounds 25–26: Sc in each st around. (48 sts)

Change to beige yarn.

Round 27: Sc in each st around. (48 sts)

Change to light brown yarn.

Round 28: Bpsc in each st around. (48 sts)

Rounds 29–30: Sc in each st around. (48 sts)

Change to beige yarn.

Round 31: Sc in each st around. (48 sts)

Change to light brown yarn.

Round 32: Bpsc in each st around. (48 sts)

Round 33: Sc in each st around. (48 sts)

Round 34: *Sc in next 6 sts, sc2tog; rep from * around. (42 sts)

Change to beige yarn.

Round 35: Sc in each st around. (42 sts)

Change to light brown yarn and begin stuffing the body.

Round 36: Bpsc in each st around. (42 sts)

Change to beige yarn.

Round 37: Sc in each st around. (42 sts)

Round 38: *Sc in next 5 sts, sc2tog; rep from * around. (36 sts)

Round 39: Sc in each st around. (36 sts)

Round 40: *Sc in next 4 sts, sc2tog; rep from * around. (30 sts)

Round 41: Sc in each st around. (36 sts)

Round 42: *Sc in next 3 sts, sc2tog; rep from * around. (24 sts)

Round 43: Sc in each st around. (24 sts)

Round 44: *Sc in next st, sc2tog; rep from * around. (16 sts)

Round 45: Sc in each st around. (16 sts)

Finish stuffing

Round 46: Sc2tog around. (8 sts)

Fasten off; weave the tail through the front loops of the last 8 sts, and pull tight to close the hole. Weave in the end.

TAIL SEGMENTS (MAKE 4 YELLOW, 1 DARK BROWN)

With dark brown/yellow yarn and size 7 hook, make a magic ring.

Round 1: 6 sc in ring. (6 sts)

Round 2: 2 sc in each st around. (12 sts)

Round 3: *Sc in next st, 2 sc in next st; rep from * around. (18 sts)

Round 4: *Sc in next 2 sts, 2 sc in next st; rep from * around. (24 sts)

Round 5: Sc in each st around. (24 sts)

Round 6: *Sc in next 5 sts, 2 sc in next st; rep from * around. (28 sts)

Rounds 7–10: Sc in each st around. (28 sts)

Round 11: *Sc in next 5 sts, sc2tog; rep from * around. (24 sts)

Sl st in next st to even out round; fasten off, leaving a long tail of yarn for assembly.

STINGER

With brown yarn and size G–6 hook, make a magic ring.

Round 1: 5 sc in ring. (5 sts)

Round 2: 2 sc in next st, sc in next 4 sts. (6 sts)

Round 3–5: Sc in each st around. (6 sts)

Round 6: Sc in next 2 sts, 2 sc in each of next 3 sts, sc in next st. (9 sts)

Round 7: Sc in next 2 sts, [2 sc in next st, sc in next st] 3 times, sc in last st. (12 sts)

Change to yellow yarn and size 7 hook.

Round 8: *Sc in next st, 2 sc in next st; rep from * around. (18 sts)

Round 9: Sc in next 3 sts, [sc in next st, 2 sc in next st] 3 times, sc in next 3 sts. (24 sts)

Round 10: Sc in each st around. (24 sts)

Round 11: *Sc in next 5 sts, 2 sc in next st; rep from * around. (28 sts)

Rounds 12–15: Sc in each st around. (28 sts)

Round 16: *Sc in next 5 sts, sc2tog; rep from * around. (24 sts)

Sl st in next st to even out round; fasten off, leaving long tail.

LEGS (MAKE 8)

With yellow yarn and size 7 hook, make a magic ring.

Round 1: 6 sc in ring. (6 sts)

Round 2: 2 sc in each st around. (12 sts)

Round 3: *Sc in next 2 sts, 2 sc in next st; rep from * around. (16 sts)

Rounds 4–6: Sc in each st around. (16 sts)

Round 7: *Sc in next 2 sts, sc2tog; rep from * around. (12 sts)

Stuff foot.

Round 8: Sc2tog around. (6 sts)

Round 9: Sc2tog around. (3 sts)

Finish as follows:

Normal leg (make 4): Ch 14; sc in 2nd ch from hook, sl st in next ch and in each ch to end. Sl st in top of foot (round 9). Fasten off.

Medium-long leg (make 2): Ch 17; sc in 2nd ch from hook, sl st in next ch and in each ch to end. Sl st in top of foot (round 9). Fasten off.

Long leg (make 2): Ch 20; sc in 2nd ch from hook, sl st in next ch and in each ch to end. Sl st in top of foot (round 9). Fasten off.

EYES (MAKE 2)

With black yarn and size G–6 hook, make a magic ring.

Round 1: 6 sc in ring. (6 sts)

Change to dark blue yarn.

Round 2: Work 2 sc in each st around. (12 sts)

Change to white yarn.

Rounds 3–4: Sc in each st around. (12 sts)

Sl st in next st to even out round; fasten off, leaving a long tail.

EYELIDS (MAKE 2)

With light brown yarn and size 7 hook, ch 9.

Row 1: Sc in 2nd ch from hook, hdc in next ch, 2 dc in next ch, dc in next 2 chs, 2 dc in next ch, hdc in next ch, 3 sc in last ch. Turn piece and work in the unused loops along the other side of the chain: Hdc in 2nd ch from hook and next 5 chs, sc in last ch, sl st in same ch. (20 sts)

Fasten off, leaving a long tail.

PINCERS (MAKE 2)

With yellow yarn and size G–6 hook, make a magic ring.

Round 1: 6 sc in ring. (6 sts)

Rounds 2–6: Sc in each st around.

Break yarn but do not fasten off; set claw aside for later. Repeat rounds 1–6 to make a second claw just like the first, but do not break the yarn. Now it's time to crochet the two parts together.

Round 7: Holding the two pieces together, start by crocheting into the first claw you made: [sc in next 2 sts, 2 sc in next st] twice. Jump back onto the second claw and work: [sc in next 2 sts, 2 sc in next st] twice. You now have a total of 16 sts going around both claws, with the beginning of the round between the two claws.

Round 8: Sc in each st around. (16 sts)

Round 9: *Sc in next 3 sts, sc2tog, sc in next 3 sts; rep from * around. (14 sts)

Round 10: Sc in each st around. (14 sts)

Round 11: *Sc in next 3 sts, sc2tog, sc in next 3 sts; rep from * around. (12 sts)

Round 12: Sc in each st around. (12 sts)

Round 13: *Sc in next 2 sts, sc2tog; rep from * around. (9 sts)

Round 14: *Sc in next st, sc2tog; rep from * around. (6 sts)

Rounds 15–26: Sc in each st around. (6 sts)

Round 27: Sc2tog around. (3 sts)

Sl st in next st to even out round; fasten off, leaving a long tail.

FINISHING

Attach the eight legs to the lower sides of the scorpion's body using yellow yarn. Start by placing the longest legs right in front of the first body segment, then the medium long legs in front of the first, and finally the two pairs of normal legs.

Sew the eyes to the sides of the head using white yarn. Don't worry if the color changes in the eyes look a little messy or uneven; turn the eye so the color changes are in the top half, and the eyelids will cover them.

Place the eyelids over the eyes, with the side with the dcs on the top. Sew in place along the top edge. Do not sew the eyelids to the eye itself; the edge of the hdc row should be free.

Embroider mouth with red yarn.

Attach the pincers between the front pair of legs and the corners of the mouth.

Place a yellow tail segment at the back end of the scorpion's body so that it covers the last couple of rounds. The front edge of the tail segment should be about 5 rounds from the last body segment. Stuff very firmly (this piece has to hold the whole tail upright) as you sew the piece in place.

Put another yellow tail segment on top of the first, making sure to cover the beginning rounds. The front edge of the cup should be 4 rounds above the body. Stuff firmly and sew.

Continue stacking the tail segments in this way—four yellow, then the dark brown segment, and finally the stinger. Make sure the yarn tail is at the bottom of the stinger piece, facing the scorpion's back; this will ensure that the stinger points the right way up.

You might find it helpful to pin all the pieces in place first, before sewing.

Weave in ends.

How can something so sweet looking be so dangerous?

Spider

Designed by Masha Pogorielova • (http://www.mashutkalu.etsy.com)

Ever have one of those mornings when it's impossible to find a pair of socks that match? Now imagine if you had eight feet to find socks for! It's no wonder this spider looks a bit frazzled. The socks in this project are a great way to use up tiny leftover amounts of bright-colored yarn.

Bulky · **Light**

YARN
Bulky-weight eyelash, mohair, or other textured yarn in black (see note on p. 83)
Regular DK-weight yarn in black
Small amount of DK-weight yarn in white
Small amounts of DK-weight yarn in assorted colors for socks

HOOK
Size B-1 (2.25 mm) crochet hook
Steel crochet hook #4 (1.25 mm)

NOTIONS
Polyester fiberfill
Yarn needle
4 pipe cleaners (optional)

FINISHED MEASUREMENTS
7 inches wide; 4 1/2 inches tall

Note
If the spider is going to live with a small child, do not use the pipe cleaners, just stuff the legs firmly while crocheting.

Adapting the pattern for different kinds of yarn

Yarn lines come and go. If you can't find black eyelash yarn, you can add fuzz yourself. Work the whole body in the regular black yarn, working through the front loops only in rounds 2–11. After the body is finished, thread short pieces of black yarn through the unworked loops on the top of the body and secure each piece with a double knot. Comb them out to make them fluffy.

PATTERN

BODY

With novelty yarn and larger hook, ch 2.

Round 1: Work 6 sc in second ch from hook. (6 sts)

Round 2: Starting with the first st of round 1 to work around in a spiral, work 2 sc in each st around. (12 sts)

Round 3: *Sc in next st, 2 sc in next st; rep from * around. (18 sts)

Round 4: *Sc in next 2 sts, 2 sc in next st; rep from * around. (24 sts)

Round 5: *Sc in next 3 sts, 2 sc in next st; rep from * around. (30 sts)

Round 6: *Sc in next 4 sts, 2 sc in next st; rep from * around. (36 sts)

Round 7: *Sc in next 5 sts, 2 sc in next st; rep from * around. (42 sts)

Round 8: *Sc in next 6 sts, 2 sc in next st; rep from * around. (48 sts)

Rounds 9–11: Sc in each st around.

Fasten off.

Turn piece inside out and join main black yarn to work in the other direction (top of body is inside out; bottom is right side out). Switch to smaller hook.

Rounds 12–15: Sc in each st around.

Round 16: *Sc in next 6 sts, sc2tog; rep from * around. (42 sts)

If you are going to use pipe cleaners, insert them now. (If the toy is for a small child, omit the pipe cleaners.)

Place two pipe cleaners together and twist their middles together a few times. This will help prevent the legs from slipping out of the body.

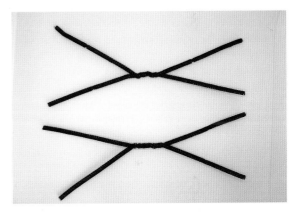

Push the ends of the legs through the second round of the regular black yarn, leaving 4 sts between every two legs on each side of the body and about 10 sts at the spider's back. You will get a little bigger gap between the front legs for the spider's head. You may find it easier to partially stuff the body before putting the legs in.

With the legs inserted into the body piece, continue to crochet the body, bending the legs back out of the way.

Round 17: *Sc in next 5 sts, sc2tog; rep from * around. (36 sts)

Round 18: *Sc in next 4 sts, sc2tog; rep from * around. (30 sts)

If you haven't stuffed the body yet, do it now.

Round 19: *Sc in next 3 sts, sc2tog; rep from * around. (24 sts)

Round 20: *Sc in next 2 sts, sc2tog; rep from * around. (18 sts)

Round 21: *Sc in next st, sc2tog; rep from * around. (12 sts)

Fasten off, leaving a long tail. Finish stuffing the body, then thread the tail through the remaining sts, tighten opening, and fasten off.

Bend the ends of the pipe cleaners back on themselves for about half an inch so the ends aren't sharp.

LEGS (MAKE 8)

With regular black yarn and smaller hook, ch 2.

Round 1: Work 6 sc in second ch from hook.

Round 2: Starting with the first st of round 1 to work around in a spiral, sc in each st around. (6 sts)

Round 3: Sc in each st around.

Round 4: Hdc in next 2 sts, sc in next st, sl st in next 2 sts, sc in next st. (6 sts)

Round 5: Hdc in next 2 sts, sc in next 4 sts. (6 sts)

Rounds 6–17: Sc in each st around.

Round 18: Sc in next 3 sts, hdc in next 2 sts, sc in next st.

Round 19: Sl st in next 2 sts, sc in next st, hdc in next 2 sts, sc in next st.

Rounds 20–31: Sc in each st around. Fasten off.

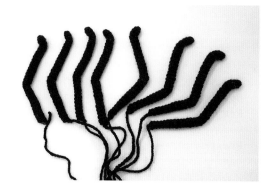

If you are not using pipe cleaners in your legs, then you will need to stuff the legs firmly so they retain their shape. It is easiest to do this as you crochet them, adding a little more stuffing every few rounds.

Slide the legs onto the pipe cleaners and sew them to the body. (Or, if not using pipe cleaners, give the legs a little extra stuffing and sew them to the body just underneath the last round of novelty yarn, distributed 2 sts apart, with larger gaps on each end for the head and the back of the body.)

HEAD

With regular black yarn and smaller hook, ch 2.

Round 1: Work 6 sc in second ch from hook.

Round 2: Starting with the first st of round 1 to work around in a spiral, work 2 sc in each st around. (12 sts)

Round 3: *Sc in next st, 2 sc in next st; rep from * around. (18 sts)

Round 4: *Sc in next 2 sts, 2 sc in next st; rep from * around. (24 sts)

Round 5: *Sc in next 3 sts, 2 sc in next st; rep from * around. (30 sts)

Round 6: *Sc in next 4 sts, 2 sc in next st; rep from * around. (36 sts)

Round 7: *Sc in next 5 sts, 2 sc in next st; rep from * around. (42 sts)

Rounds 8–12: Sc in each st around.

Round 13: *Sc in next 5 sts, sc2tog; rep from * around. (36 sts)

Sl st in next st to even out round, then fasten off.

SMALL EYE

With white and smaller hook, ch 2.

Round 1: Work 6 sc in second ch from hook.

Round 2: Starting with the first st of round 1 to work around in a spiral, work 2 sc in each st around. (12 sts)

Round 3: *Sc in next st, 2 sc in next st; rep from * around. (18 sts)

Round 4: Sc in each st around.

Sl st in next st to even out round, then fasten off.

SMALL PUPIL

With regular black yarn and smaller hook, ch 2.

Round 1: Work 6 sc in second ch from hook.

Work 1 sc in first st of round 1; sl st in next st; fasten off.

LARGE EYE

With white and smaller hook, ch 2.

Round 1: Work 6 sc in second ch from hook.

Round 2: Starting with the first st of round 1 to work around in a spiral, work 2 sc in each st around. (12 sts)

Round 3: *Sc in next st, 2 sc in next st; rep from * around. (18 sts)

Round 4: *Sc in next 2 sts, 2 sc in next st; rep from * around. (24 sts)

Round 5: Sc in each st around.

Sl st in next st to even out round, then fasten off.

LARGE PUPIL

With regular black yarn and smaller hook, ch 2.

Round 1: Work 6 sc in second ch from hook.

Round 2: Starting with the first st of round 1 to work around in a spiral, work 2 sc in next 5 sts, sl st in next st.

Fasten off.

FINISHING

Sew the pupils to the eyes with wrong sides out. Highlight the pupils with a few stitches with white yarn (see photo). Sew the eyes together, then sew the eyes to the upper part of the head, just above the middle. Stuff the eyes firmly as you sew them to the head.

Stuff the head and sew it to the body in the widest gap between the legs, a little higher than halfway up the side of the body (so that the top of the head is sewn to the fluffy part and the bottom edge to the plain part). Weave in all ends.

SOCKS (MAKE 8)

> ### Note
>
> To change colors smoothly, insert the hook into the last st of color A, yarn over with A, and draw up a loop. Then yarn over with B and draw up the loop of B through the two loops of A on the hook.

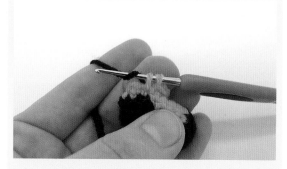

Continue in rounds.

Rounds 9–10: With B, sc in each st around.

Rounds 11–15: With any color of your choice, sc in each st around.

Sl st in next st to even out round, then fasten off. Weave in ends.

With color A and smaller hook, ch 2.

Round 1: Work 6 sc in second ch from hook.

Round 2: Starting with the first st of round 1 to work around in a spiral, work 2 sc in each st around. (12 sts)

Rounds 3–4: Sc in each st around, changing to color B in last st of round 4.

Rounds 5–8: With B, sc in each st around, changing to color A in last st of round 8.

Turn Heel: With A, sl st in next st, ch 1, turn.

Continue in rows:

Rows 1–5: Sk sl st, sc in next 5 sts, sl st in next st, ch 1, turn.

Round 6: Sk sl st, sc in next 6 sts, changing to color B in last st.

Eight socks, and none of them match!

Tick

Designed by Susan K. Burkhart • (http://www.OohLookItsARabbit.etsy.com)

Ticks are often confused with insects, but they are actually arachnids, having eight legs instead of six—as you can clearly see in this larger-than-life version. This particular tick is a Lone Star Tick, *Amblyomma americanum*—a female (males lack the large white spot). "Living on property surrounded by woods," the designer says, "my husband and I manage to attract quite a few of these critters each summer. I hope you enjoy making your own little bloodsucker."

4 Medium

YARN
Worsted-weight yarn in dark brown (approximately 2 oz) and white (scrap amount)

HOOK
Size F-5 (3.75 mm) crochet hook

NOTIONS
Two 6 mm black glass or onyx beads for eyes
1 yard of cotton rope or cord (1/8 in. in diameter)
Black upholstery thread
Polyester fiberfill

> Substitute embroidery for the bead eyes if the toy is meant for young children.

FINISHED MEASUREMENTS
Body 5 inches long (including mouthparts);
9 inches wide (including legs)

PATTERN

HEAD AND BODY

Using dark brown yarn

Start with a magic ring.

Round 1: Work 5 sc into ring (OR ch 2, work 5 sc in second ch from hook). (5 sts)

Round 2: Starting in the 1st st of rnd 1 and working in a continuous spiral, sc in each st around. (5 sts)

Rounds 3–6: Sc in each st around. (5 sts)

Round 7: 3 sc in first st, sc in next 2 sts, 3 sc in next st, sc in next st. (9 sts)

Stuff mouth part at this point if desired. Depending on the type of yarn used, it may be stiff enough to hold its shape without stuffing.

Round 8: 2 sc in each of next 3 sts, sc in next 2 sts, 2 sc in each of next 3 sts, sc in last st. (15 sts)

Round 9: [Sc in next 3 sts, 2 sc in each of next 3 sts] 2 times, sc in next 3 sts. (21 sts)

Round 10: [sc in next 4 sts, 2 sc in each of next 4 sts] 2 times, sc in next 5 sts. (29 sts)

Round 11: Sc in next 7 sts, 2 sc in each of next 2 sts, sc in next 10 sts, 2 sc in each of next 2 sts, sc in next 8 sts. (33 sts)

Rounds 12–14: Sc in each st around. (33 sts)

Round 15: Sc in next 8 sts, 2 sc in each of next 2 sts, sc in next 15 sts, 2 sc in each of next 2 sts, sc in next 6 sts. (37 sts)

Round 16: Sc in next 9 sts, 2 sc in each of next 2 sts, sc in next 17 sts, 2 sc in each of next 2 sts, sc in next 7 sts. (41 sts)

Round 17–28: Sc in each st around. (41 sts)

Round 29: Sc in next 13 sts, sc2tog 3 times, sc in next 14 sts, sc2tog 3 times, sc in next 2 sts. (35 sts)

Round 30: Sc in each st around. (35 sts)

Round 31: Sc in next 11 sts, sc2tog 3 times, sc in next 12 sts, sc2tog 3 times. (29 sts)

Round 32: Sc2tog, sc in next 8 sts, sc2tog 3 times, sc in next 9 sts, sc2tog 2 times. (23 sts)

Round 33: Sc in each st around. (23 sts)

Stuff body somewhat firmly, while maintaining as flat a body as possible. Continue to add stuffing as needed as you work the final rounds of the body.

Round 34: Sc2tog 2 times, sc in next 3 sts, sc2tog 4 times, sc in next 4 sts, sc2tog 2 times. (15 sts)

Round 35: Sc2tog 2 times, sc in next 2 sts, sc2tog 3 times, sc in next st, sc2tog. (9 sts)

Round 36: Sc2tog 2 times, sc in next st, sc2tog 2 times. (5 sts)

Sl st in next st, fasten off. Sew up opening and pull end of yarn into body.

SIDE MOUTHPARTS (MAKE 2)

With dark brown yarn, start with a magic ring.

Round 1: Work 5 sc in ring (OR ch 2, work 5 sc in second ch from hook). (5 sts)

Round 2: Starting in the 1st st of round 1 and working in a continuous spiral, sc in each st around. (5 sts)

Rounds 3–7: Sc in each st around. (5 sts)

Sl st in next st, then fasten off, leaving enough yarn to sew onto head. Stuff if desired.

Sew one side mouthpart onto each side of the central mouthpart.

BODY SPOT (MAKE 1)

With white yarn, start with a magic ring.

Round 1: Work 6 sc in ring (OR ch 2, work 6 sc in second ch from hook). (6 sts)

Round 2: Starting in the 1st st of round 1 and working in a continuous spiral, 2 sc in every st around. (12 sts)

Sl st in next st and fasten off, leaving enough yarn to sew onto back of body.

LEGS (MAKE 8)

With dark brown yarn, ch 21, leaving about 12" of yarn at the beginning of the chain.

Row 1: Sc in 2nd ch from hook and each remaining ch; ch 1 and turn. (20 sts)

Row 2–3: Sc in each st across; ch 1 and turn. (20 sts)

Fold rectangle in half lengthwise. Insert a length of cotton cord inside the tube formed.

Row 4: Sc rows 1 and 3 together as follows: *Insert hook through next sc of row 3 and corresponding ch loop of row 1, yarn over and draw up a loop (2 loops on hook), yarn over and pull through both loops on hook; rep from * across. (20 sts)

You will now have a long tube with a piece of cord encased inside it.

Fasten off, leaving enough yarn to sew the leg onto the body. Use the yarn left at the beginning of the leg to sew the end of the tube closed.

FINISHING

Sew 4 legs onto each side of body. Orient the legs so that the ridge created from crocheting rows 1 and 3 together faces the direction you want the legs to curve. I curved the first pair of legs toward the head, and the remaining 3 pairs of legs away from the head.

Sew beads onto head using upholstery thread, pulling tight to recess beads into head.

Ready for my close-up!

Slug

Designed by Stacey Trock • (http://www.freshstitches.com)

In real life, slugs can be a little bit slimy . . . but not this cuddly one! Isn't she adorably irresistible? Crochet her up in a yellow yarn to make a banana slug, or pick a more classic gray for the traditional coloring.

YARN
Worsted-weight yarn in yellow (35 yards) and white (10 yards)

4 Medium

HOOK
Size G-6 (4 mm) crochet hook

NOTIONS
Yarn needle
Polyester fiberfill
Two 12 mm black animal eyes

FINISHED MEASUREMENTS
4 inches tall; 5^1/$_2$ inches long

PATTERN

Note

Crochet through the back loop only,
unless otherwise directed.

ANTENNAE (MAKE 2)
With yellow, ch 2.

Round 1: Work 6 sc in 2nd ch from hook. (6 sts)

Round 2: Starting with the first st of round 1 to work in the round, sc in each st around. (6 sts)

Rounds 3–8: Sc in each st around. (6 sts)
Fasten off, leaving a long tail.

EYES (MAKE 2)
With white, ch 2.

Round 1: Work 6 sc in 2nd ch from hook. (6 sts)

Round 2: Starting with the first st of round 1 to work in the round, work 2 sc in each st around. (12 sts)

Round 3: *2 sc in next st, sc in next st; rep from * around. (18 sts)

Rounds 4–5: Sc in each st around. (18 sts)

Round 6: *Sc2tog, sc in next st; rep from * around. (12 sts)

Fasten off, leaving a long tail.

Fasten a plastic eye to round 4 of each crocheted eye by inserting the post of each eye between two stitches and pressing the washer onto the back post to secure the eye.

BODY
With yellow, ch 2.

Round 1: Work 6 sc in 2nd ch from hook. (6 sts)

Round 2: Starting with the first st of round 1 to work in the round, work 2 sc in each st around. (12 sts)

Round 3: *2 sc in next st, sc in next st; rep from * around. (18 sts)

Round 4: *2 sc in next st, sc in next 2 sts; rep from * around. (24 sts)

Round 5: *2 sc in next st, sc in next 3 sts; rep from * around. (30 sts)

Rounds 6–10: Sc in each st around. (30 sts)

Round 11: *Sc2tog, sc in next 3 sts; rep from * around. (24 sts)

Rounds 12–14: Sc in each st around. (24 sts)

Round 15: *Sc2tog, sc in next 2 sts; rep from * around. (18 sts)

Rounds 16–19: Sc in each st around. (18 sts)
Remove hook, but do not fasten off.

Stuff eyes and attach to rounds 5–6 of body.

Attach antennae to rounds 6–7 of body, one antennae centered directly behind each eye.

Stuff body.
Continue crocheting where you left off.

Round 20: *Sc2tog, sc in next st; rep from * around. (12 sts)

Rounds 21–23: Sc in each st around. (12 sts)
Shove in a little more stuffing!

Round 24: Sc2tog around. (6 sts)

Round 25: Sc next st and 4th st together. (1)
Fasten off, pulling knot to the inside of the project.

FOOT

She's a beautiful-looking slug, isn't she? But she's not done yet! To make the sluggy-foot, single crochet around the bottom of your slug, as follows:

Round 1: Join a strand of MC to the front loop of a stitch on the bottom edge with a single crochet.

Continue around, single crocheting in the front loop (as pictured) of each stitch on the bottom edge of the slug.

There's no exact formula or number of stitches you should end up with—what's important is that you end up with an oval of stitches (as pictured) that go around the bottom of your slug.

Sit your slug on her foot, and see if she sits up nicely. If not, you may want to rip out part of the first round and adjust the placement or number of stitches accordingly.

Round 2: Work 2 sc in each stitch around. Fasten off. Weave in ends.

Wormy Apple

Designed by CAROCreated/Carola Herbst • (http://www.etsy.com/de/shop/CAROcreated)

Usually finding a worm in an apple is a bad experience (rivaled only by finding half a worm)—but in this case, the worm is so cute, it's hard to object! Take your time as you make this project; the crocheting isn't terribly difficult, but it's important to go carefully so that you end up with an empty hole through the middle of the apple. When you're finished, the worm will be able to crawl in and out of the apple.

YARN

1 Super Fine

Fingering-weight cotton yarn in green (one ball plus a very small separate ball of the same color), yellow, white, and small amounts of brown and dark green

HOOK

Size B-1 (2.25 mm) crochet hook [2.5 mm doesn't exist in the American sizing system, so I went with the closest smaller size]

NOTIONS

Polyester fiberfill
2 black beads, 4 mm in diameter
1 white pipe cleaner (approximately 20 in. long)
Black sewing thread
Long yarn needle (4 in.)
Sewing needle
Stitch marker

FINISHED MEASUREMENTS

Apple 3 inches tall; 10^1/$_2$ inches around; worm 8 inches long

SPECIAL STITCH

Crochet from the wrong side: Insert your hook into the stitch from back to front (instead of front to back as you normally would).

Yarn over, and pull up a loop.

Finish the sc as normal.

PATTERN

WORM

With yellow, make a magic ring.

Round 1: Work 6 sc in magic ring. (6 sts)

Round 2: Work 2 sc in each st around. (12 sts)

Round 3: *Sc in next 2 sts, 2 sc in next st; rep from * around. (16 sts)

Round 4–6: Sc in each st around. (16 sts)

Round 7: Sc2tog 4 times, sc in next 8 sts. (12 sts)

Round 8: Sc in next 8 sts, sc2tog, sc in next 2 sts. (11 sts)

Round 9: Sc in next 2 sts, sc2tog, sc in next 7 sts. (10 sts)

Fold the pipe cleaner in half and twist tightly. Insert the pipe cleaner into the worm with the blunt (folded) end in the worm's head after a few rows and stuff around it as you crochet the rest of the worm.

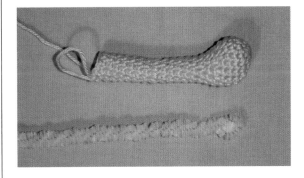

Round 10–35: Sc in each st around. (10 sts)

Round 36: Sc2tog, sc in next 8 sts. (9 sts)

Round 37–38: Sc in each st around. (9 sts)

Round 39: Sc in next 3 sts, sc2tog, sc in next 4 sts. (8 sts)

Round 40–41: Sc in each st around. (8 sts)

Round 42: Sc in next 5 sts, sc2tog, sc in next st. (7 sts)

Round 43–44: Sc in each st around. (7 sts)

Round 45: Sc in next 2 sts, sc2tog, sc in next 3 sts. (6 sts)

Round 46–47: Sc in each st around. (6 sts)

Round 48: Sc2tog, sc in next 4 sts. (5 sts)

Round 49–50: Sc in each st around. (5 sts)

Fasten off, leaving a long tail. Cut the ends of the pipe cleaner and fold over the tips.

Close the small hole that remains in the end. Weave in the loose end.

FINISHING

With black sewing thread and a sewing needle, sew a bead to each side of the head, approximately between rounds 3 and 4.

APPLE

With green, make a magic ring.

Round 1: Work 6 sc in magic ring. (6 sts)

Round 2: *2 sc in next st, sc in next st; rep from * around. (9 sts)

Round 3: Sc in each st around. (9 sts)

Round 4: 2 sc in each st around. (18 sts)

Round 5: *2 sc in next st, sc in next 2 sts; rep from * around. (24 sts)

Round 6: *Sc in next 2 sts, 2 sc in next st, sc in next st; rep from * around. (30 sts)

Round 7: *Sc in next 4 sts, 2 sc in next st; rep from * around. (36 sts)

Round 8: *Sc in next st, 2 sc in next st, sc in next 4 sts; rep from * around. (42 sts)

Round 9: *Sc in next 4 sts, 2 sc in next st, sc in next 2 sts; rep from *around. (48 sts)

Round 10: *Sc in next 7 sts, 2 sc in next st; rep from * around. (54 sts)

Round 11: *Sc in next 3 sts, 2 sc in next st, sc in next 5 sts; rep from * around. (60 sts)

Round 12–16: Sc in each st around. (60 sts)

Round 17: Sc in next 58 sts, sl st in next 2 sts. (60 sts)

Round 18: Sc in next 56 sts, sc2tog. (57 sts)

Now continue in rows for the worm hole.

Row 19: Ch 1, turn; working from back to front through both loops of each st, sc in next 55 sts, sc2tog. (56 sts)

Row 20: Ch 1, turn; working sts normally, sc in next 56 sts. (56 sts)

Row 21: Ch 1, turn; working from back to front, sc in next 56 sts. (56 sts)

Row 22: Ch 1, turn; working sts normally, work 2 sc in next st, sc in next 54 sts, 2 sc in next st, ch 2. (60 sts)

Do not turn; continue in rounds.

Round 23: Sc in each st around. (60 sts)

Round 24: Sc in next 23 sts, sl st in next 2 sts, sc in next 35 sts. (60 sts)

Round 25: Sc in next 21 sts, sc2tog.

Continue in rows for the second worm hole.

Row 26: Ch 1, turn; working from back to front, sc in next 5 sts, sc2tog. (56 sts)

Row 27: Ch 1, turn; working sts normally, sc in next 6 sts, [sc2tog, sc in next 12 sts] 3 times, sc2tog, sc in next 6 sts. (52 sts)

Row 28: Ch 1, turn; working from back to front, sc in next 52 sts. (52 sts)

Row 29: Ch 1, turn; working sts normally, work 2 sc in next st, sc in next 50 sts, 2 sc in next st, ch 2. (56 sts)

Do not turn; continue in rounds.

Round 30: Sc in next 6 sts, [sc2tog, sc in next 12 sts] 3 times, sc2tog, sc in next 6 sts. (52 sts)

Rounds 31–32: Sc in each st around. (52 sts)

Stop work at this point but do not fasten off. Put your working loop on a locking marker or pull it larger (before you cut the yarn) so your work doesn't pull out while you work on the next part—the connection between the two holes.

WORM HOLE

With right side facing out, join the second ball of green yarn in the edge of one of the holes.

Round 1: 14 sc around edge. (14 sts)

Break off green and join white.

Rounds 2–11: Sc in each st around. (14 sts)

Fasten off and weave in all ends.

Repeat with the other hole. Fasten off, leaving a long tail.

Turn the entire piece inside out and allign the ends of the tubes, being careful not to twist. Sew the tubes together with the long tail from the second one to form a single tunnel through the center of the apple. Weave in all ends.

APPLE FINISHING

Pick up where you left off after round 32.

Round 33: *Sc in next 11 sts, sc2tog; rep from * around. (48 sts)

Round 34: Sc in each st around. (48 sts)

Round 35: *Sc in next 6 sts, sc2tog; rep from * around. (42 sts)

Round 36: Sc in each st around. (42 sts)

Round 37: *Sc in next 2 sts, sc2tog, sc in next 3 sts; rep from * around. (36 sts)

Round 38: *Sc in next 3 sts, sc2tog, sc in next st; rep from * around. (30 sts)

Insert the worm into the tunnel to keep the tube from getting crushed. Stuff the apple firmly with fiberfill.

Round 39: *Sc2tog, sc in next 3 sts; rep from * around. (24 sts)

Round 40: *Sc in next 2 sts, sc2tog; rep from * around. (18 sts)

Round 41: *Sc2tog, sc in next st; rep from * around. (12 sts)

Stuff the remaining apple with fiberfill.

Round 42: Sc2tog around. (6 sts)

Fasten off, leaving a long tail. Use the tail to close up the small hole that remains. To shape the apple, thread the long tail into a long tapestry needle and insert the needle several times from the bottom to the top of the apple and back from top to bottom again. Pull tight. Make sure you don't sew through the worm hole tube (and the worm). Carefully secure the yarn tail. Weave in the loose end.

STEM

With brown, ch 13, leaving a 12" tail at the beginning.

Row 1: Sl st in 2nd ch from hook and in each st across. Ch 1, turn piece around, and continue along the back of the foundation ch, working 1 sl st in each ch across. Fasten off, leaving a 13" tail.

Use a yarn needle to weave the fasten-on yarn tail through the stem so you have both yarn tails on one side. Knot the yarn tails together.

LEAF

With dark green, ch 10.

Row 1: Sc in 2nd ch from hook, sc in next ch, hdc in next ch, dc in next 4 chs, hdc in next ch, [sc, ch 2, sc] in last ch; turn work and continue along the back of the foundation chain as follows: hdc in next ch, dc in next 4 chs, sc in next 2 chs, sl st in beg sc.

Fasten off, leaving a long tail.

FINISHING

Use the long tail of the leaf to sew the leaf to the stem. Weave in ends.

Thread one of the yarn tails on the stem through a yarn needle and insert needle through the apple from top to bottom (avoiding the worm and its hole). Pull the end of the yarn tail out through the center of the bottom of the apple. Repeat for the other yarn tail. Tie the two tails together and trim the ends. Tie on a few more strands of yarn to form the remnants of the apple blossom.

A perfect gift for a favorite teacher.

Frog

Designed by Mevlinn Gusick • (http://www.mevvsan.com)

It's not easy being green, as the famous song goes, and this little guy seems to know it. Sit him on the edge of a shelf or a computer monitor for a little reminder that things could be worse! The tops of the frog's legs are sewn to his bottom and help to stabilize him as he sits; if he's a little unsteady, adjust the placement of the legs a bit.

YARN
Worsted-weight yarn in green and white

HOOK
Size C-2 (2.75 mm) crochet hook

NOTIONS
Yarn needle
Polyester fiberfill
6 mm safety eyes

FINISHED MEASUREMENTS
2$\frac{1}{2}$ tall (not including legs)

PATTERN

BODY

With green, make a magic ring.

Round 1: 6 sc in ring. (6 sts) Mark the end of the round but do not join; continue in a spiral throughout body.

Round 2: 2 sc tbl in each st around. (12 sts)

Round 3: *2 sc tbl in next st, sc tbl in next st; repeat from * around. (18 sts)

Rounds 4–6: Sc tbl in each st around. (18 sts)

Round 7: Sc2tog tbl in first st. Sc tbl in next st and in each st around. (17 sts)

Round 8: Sc tbl in each st around. (17 sts)

Round 9: *Sc2tog tbl, sc tbl in next 2 sts; repeat from * around. (12 sts)

Round 10: Sc tbl in each st around. (12 sts)

Stuff body.

Round 11: *Sc2tog tbl, sc tbl in next st; repeat from * around. (6 sts)

Round 12: Sc2tog tbl around. Fasten off.

Before you stuff and close up the body, make sure you have the piece turned wrong-side-out so that the ridges from crocheting through the back loops are on the inside of the piece.

ARMS (MAKE 2)

Ch 9.

Sc in fourth ch from hook (first finger formed).

Ch 3, sc into the same ch as first sc (second finger).

Ch 3, sc into the same ch as before again (third finger).

Sl st in next ch and in each ch to end of foundation ch. Fasten off.

FEET (MAKE 2)

Ch 19.

Sc into the fifth ch from hook (first toe formed).

Ch 4, sc into same ch as first sc (second toe).

Ch 4, sc into the same ch again (third toe).

Sl st in next ch and in each ch to end of foundation ch. Fasten off.

EYES (MAKE 2)

Make a magic ring.

Round 1: 4 sc in ring.

Push the front of the safety eye through the center of the magic ring. With the eye in the ring, put the back of the eye on.

Round 2: Sc tbl in each st. (4 sts) Fasten off.

FINISHING

Sew the arms to each side of the frog, a little higher than halfway up. Sew the legs to the frog's bottom. Sew the eyes on each side of the head.

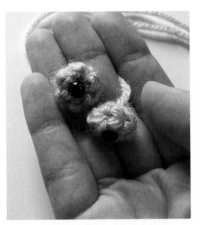

Snail

Designed by Wendy Thornburg • (http://www.drunkenauntwendydesigns.wordpress.com)

T his snail sports an impressively ruffled shell, but don't be scared off! All the complicated-looking ruffles are made by simple increases and decreases. This pattern is a nice halfway point between whimsical and realistic.

YARN

Worsted-weight yarn in green, coral, and aqua (about 3.5 oz/100 g each)

HOOK

Size E-4 (3.5 mm) crochet hook

NOTIONS

Yarn needle
10.5 mm plastic safety eyes in green
Polyester fiberfill

FINISHED MEASUREMENTS

9 inches long; 8 inches tall

PATTERN

TOP OF BODY

With green, ch 26.

Round 1: Sc in 2nd ch from hook and in next 23 chs, then work 4 sc in last ch. Turn and work in unused loops along back of foundation chain: 1 sc in next 23 chs, 4 sc in last ch. (55 sts)

Round 2: 2 sc in next st, sc in next 22 sts, 2 sc in next st, sc in next 4 sts, 2 sc in next st, sc in next 22 sts, 2 sc in each of next 4 sts. (62 sts)

Round 3: Sc in next 52 sts, [sc in next st, 2 sc in next st] 5 times. (67 sts)

Round 4: Sc in next 56 sts, 2 sc in next 11 sts. (78 sts)

Rounds 5–10: Sc in each st around.

Fasten off.

BOTTOM OF BODY

With green, ch 26.

Round 1: Sc in 2nd ch from hook and in next 23 chs, then work 4 sc in last ch. Turn and work in unused loops along back of foundation chain: 1 sc in next 23 chs, 4 sc in last ch. (55 sts)

Round 2: Sc in next 24 sts, [sc in next st, 2 sc in next st] 2 times, sc in next 23 sts, [sc in next st, 2 sc in next st] 2 times. (59 sts)

Round 3: Sc in next 24 sts, [sc in next 2 sts, 2 sc in next st] 2 times, sc in next 23 sts, [sc in next 2 sts, 2 sc in next st] 2 times. (63 sts)

Round 4: Sc in next 24 sts, [sc in next 3 sts, 2 sc in next st] 2 times, sc in next 23 sts, [sc in next 3 sts, 2 sc in next st] 2 times. (67 sts)

Notes

- When changing colors work last stitch of one color until two loops remain on hook, join new color. This will make the top of the stitch stay the correct color.
- In the slip stich section, make your slip stitches loose. It will make the next row easier.
- You may prefer to run the unused colors of yarn along the inside of the piece instead of stopping and starting a new piece each time.

Round 5: Sc in next 24 sts, [sc in next 4 sts, 2 sc in next st] 2 times, sc in next 23 sts, [sc in next 4 sts, 2 sc in next st] 2 times. (71 sts)

Round 6: Sc in next 27 sts, 2 sc in each of next 5 sts, sc in next 39 sts. (76 sts)

Round 7: Sc each st tog with corresponding st of top piece, stuffing as you go.

Round 8: 2 sc in each st around. (152 sts)

Fasten off.

ANTENNAE (MAKE 2)

With green, make a magic ring.

Round 1: Work 4 sc in ring. (4 sts)

Round 2: 2 sc in each st around. (8 sts)

Rounds 3–4: Sc in each st around. Place eyes between round 3 and round 4.

Round 5: Sc2tog around. (4 sts)
Rounds 6–8: Sc in each st around.
Sl st in next st. Fasten off.
Sew to front of the body.

SHELL

Make a magic ring.
Round 1: With coral, work 4 sc in ring. (4 sts)
Round 2: Work 2 sc in each st. (8 sts)
Round 3: *Sc in next st, 2 sc in next st; rep from * around. (12 sts)
Round 4: *Sc in next 2 sts, 2 sc in next st; rep from * around, changing to aqua in last st. (16 sts)
Round 5: Sc in each st around.
Round 6: Sc2tog in each st around, changing to coral in last st. (8 sts)
Round 7: Work 2 sc in each st around. (16 sts)
Round 8: *Sc in next st, 2 sc in next st; rep from * around. (24 sts)
Round 9: *Sc in next 2 sts, 2 sc in next st; rep from * around. (32 sts)
Round 10: *Sc in next 3 sts, 2 sc in next st; rep from * around. (40 sts)
Round 11: [Sc in next 4 sts, 2 sc in next st] twice; sc next st tog with corresponding st in round 3, sc in next 3

sts, 2 sc in next st; [sc in next 4 sts, 2 sc in next st] 5 more times, changing to aqua in last st. (48 sts)

Round 12: SC in each st around.
Round 13: Sc2tog in each st around, changing to coral in last st. (24 sts)
Round 14: Work 2 sc in each st around. (48 sts)
Round 15: *Sc in next st, 2 sc in next st; rep from * around. (72 sts)
Round 16: *Sc in next 2 sts, 2 sc in next st; rep from * around. (96 sts)
Rounds 17–19: Sc in each st around.
Round 20: Rep round 17, changing to aqua in last st.
Round 21: *Sc, sc2tog; rep from * around. (64 sts)
Round 22: Sc2tog in each st around, changing to coral in last st. (32 sts)
Round 23: Work 2 sc in each of next 20 sts, sl st in next 12 sts. (40 sc, 12 sl st)
Round 24: [Sc in next st, 2 sc in next st] 20 times, sl st in next 12 sts. (60 sc, 12 sl st)
Round 25: [Sc in next 2 sts, 2 sc in next st] 20 times, sl st in next 12 sts. (80 sc, 12 sl st)
Round 26: [Sc in next 3 sts, 2 sc in next st] 20 times, sl st in next 12 sts. (100 sc, 12 sl st)
Round 27: Sc2tog twice, sc in next 92 sts, sc2tog twice, sl st in next 12 sts. (96 sc, 12 sl st)
Round 28: Sl st in next 2 sts, sc2tog twice, sc in next 84 sts, sc2tog twice, sl st in next 14 sts. (88 sc, 16 sl st)
Round 29: Sl st in next 4 sts, sc2tog twice, sc in next 76 sts, sc2tog twice, sl st in next 16 sts. (80 sc, 20 sl st)

Round 30: Sl st in next 6 sts, [sc in next 3 sts, sc2tog in next st] 15 times, sl st in next 17 sts, changing to aqua in last st. (60 sc, 23 sl st)

Round 31: Sl st in next 6 sts, [sc, sc2tog] 20 times, sc in next 2 sts, sl st in next 17 sts. (42 sc, 23 sl st)

Round 32: Sl st in next 6 sts, sc2tog 21 times, sl st in next 17 sts, changing to coral in last st. (21 sc, 23 sl st)

Round 33: Sc in each st around. (44 sc)

Round 34: Work 2 sc in each st around. (88 sts)

Round 35: Rep round 34. (176 sts)

Sl st in next st. Fasten off.

Sew to body through last aqua row, stuffing as you go. Stuff firmly to get fewer ruffles in the shell and loosely for more ruffles.

Weave in all ends.

Slow moving but still adorable!

Tarantula

Designed by Amber Perry • (http://www.AmberPerryPatterns.com)

Tarantulas are one of the more unusual pets out there, but there are many people who find them fascinating. They make good pets, too—they're quiet and don't need a lot of space, and you don't have to walk them every day or clean a litterbox. But if you're not quite sure about a real live tarantula, you might like this crocheted version—who comes with a meal (a cricket) included.

3 Light

YARN
DK-weight cotton yarn in black and gold, plus small amount of tan for cricket

HOOK
Size C-2 (2.75 mm) crochet hook

NOTIONS
Pair of 9 mm plastic safety eyes
Stitch marker
Polyester fiberfill
Yarn needle
8 pipe cleaners (optional)

FINISHED MEASUREMENTS
Spider's body 6 inches long; spider 8
    inches wide (including legs); cricket
    1³/₄ inches long

SPIDER

ABDOMEN

With black, begin with a magic loop.

Round 1: 6 sc in loop. (6 sts)

Round 2: 2 sc in each st around. (12 sts)

Round 3: *Sc in next st, 2 sc in next st; rep from * to end. (18 sts)

Round 4: *Sc in next 2 sts, 2 sc in next st; rep from * to end. (24 sts)

Round 5: *Sc in next 3 sts, 2 sc in next st; rep from * to end. (30 sts)

Round 6: *Sc in next 4 sts, 2 sc in next st; rep from * to end. (36 sts)

Round 7: *Sc in next 17 sts, 2 sc in next st; rep from * to end. (38 sts)

Round 8: *Sc in next 18 sts, 2 sc in next st; rep from * to end. (40 sts)

Round 9: Sc in each st around.

Round 10: [Sc in next 4 sts, 2 sc in next st] 4 times, sc in next 20 sts. (44 sts)

Round 11: Sc around. (44 sts)

Round 12: [Sc in next 5 sts, 2 sc in next st] 4 times, sc in next 20 sts. (48 sts)

Round 13–14: Sc in each st around. (48 sts)

Round 15: *Sc in next 10 sts, sc2tog; rep from * to end. (44 sts)

Round 16–17: Sc in each st around. (44 sts)

Round 18: *Sc in next 9 sts, sc2tog; rep from * to end. (40 sts)

Round 19: Sc in each st around. (40 sts)

Round 20: *Sc in next 8 sts, sc2tog; rep from * to end. (36 sts)

Round 21: *Sc in next 7 sts, sc2tog; rep from * to end. (32 sts)

Round 22: *Sc in next 6 sts, sc2tog; rep from * to end. (28 sts)

Begin stuffing.

Round 23: Sc in each st around. (28 sts)

Round 24: *Sc in next 5 sts, sc2tog; rep from * to end. (24 sts)

Round 25: *Sc2tog, sc in next 10 sts; rep from * to end. (22 sts)

Round 26: Sc in each st around. (22 sts)

Round 27: *Sc2tog, sc in next 9 sts; rep from * to end. (20 sts)

Round 28: Sc in each st around. (20 sts)

Round 29: *Sc in next 2 sts, sc2tog; rep from * to end. (15 sts)

Round 30: *Sc in next st, sc2tog; rep from * to end. (10 sts)

Fasten off.

SPINNERETS (MAKE 2)

Ch 6.

Row 1: Sl st in second chain from hook and each ch to end.

Fasten off and sew to back end of abdomen.

CEPHALOTHORAX (HEAD)

With black, begin with a magic loop.

Round 1: 5 sc in loop. (5 sts)

Round 2: 2 sc in each st around. (10 sts)

Round 3: *Sc in next st, 2 sc in next st; rep from * to end. (15 sts)

Round 4: *Sc in next 2 sts, 2 sc in next st; rep from * to end. (20 sts)

Round 5: *Sc in next 3 sts, 2 sc in next st; rep from * to end. (25 sts)

Round 6: *Sc in next 4 sts, 2 sc in next st; rep from * to end. (30 sts)

Round 7: *Sc in next 5 sts, 2 sc in next st; rep from * to end, changing to gold in last stitch. (35 sts)

Round 8: With gold, sc in each st around, changing to black in last stitch. (35 sts)

Round 9: With black, *sc in next 6 sts, 2 sc in next st; rep from * to end. (40 sts)

Rounds 10–11: Sc in each st around. (40 sts)

Attach safety eyes between rounds 8 and 9, with one st between eyes.

Round 12: *Sc in next 6 sts, sc2tog; rep from * to end. (35 sts)

Round 13: *Sc in next 5 sts, sc2tog; rep from * to end. (30 sts)

Round 14: *Sc in next 4 sts, sc2tog; rep from * to end. (25 sts)

Round 15: *Sc in next 3 sts, sc2tog; rep from * to end. (20 sts)

Round 16: *Sc in next 2 sts, sc2tog; rep from * to end. (15 sts)

Fasten off and sew to abdomen.

STERNUM

With black, begin with a magic loop.

Round 1: 5 sc in loop. (5 sts)

Round 2: 2 sc in each st, changing to gold in last stitch. (10 sts)

Round 3: With gold,*sc in next st, 2 sc in next st; rep from * to end. (15 sts)

Fasten off and sew to the center of the underside of the cephalothorax.

LEGS (MAKE 8)

With black, begin with a magic loop.

Round 1: 6 sc in loop. (6 sts)

Round 2: *Sc in next 2 sts, 2 sc in next st; rep from * to end. (8 sts)

Round 3–6: Sc in each st around, changing to gold in last st of round 6. (8 sts)

Round 7: With gold, sc in each st around, changing to black in last stitch. (8 sts)

Round 8–10: With black, sc in each st around, changing to gold in last st of round 10. (8 sts)

Round 11–12: With gold, sc in each st around, changing to black in last st of round 12. (8 sts)

Round 13–15: With black, sc in each st around, changing to gold in last st of round 15. (8 sts)

Round 16–18: With gold, sc in each st around, changing to black in last st of round 18. (8 sts)

Round 19–22: With black, sc in each st around, changing to gold in last st of round 22. (8 sts)

Round 23–24: With gold, sc in each st around, changing to black in last st of round 24. (8 sts)

Round 25–29: With black, sc in each st around. (8 sts) Fasten off.

Insert chenille stems into legs if desired and stuff firmly to last round of gold.

PEDIPALP (MAKE 2)

With gold, begin with a magic loop.

Round 1: 6 sc in loop. (6 sts)

Round 2–6: Sc in each st around, changing to black in last stitch of round 6. (6 sts)

Round 7–11: With black, sc in each st around. (6 sts) Fasten off and stuff.

CHELICERAE (MAKE 2)

With gold, begin with a magic loop.

Round 1: 5 sc in loop. (5 sts)

Round 2: 2 sc in each st around. (10 sts)

Round 3–4: Sc in each st around. (10 sts)

Sl st in first stitch of last round and fasten off. Stuff.

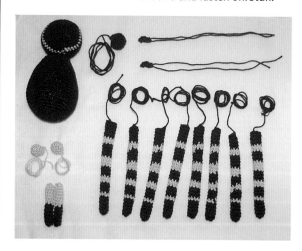

FANGS (MAKE 2)

Ch 4.

Sl st in second chain from hook, sc in next 2 ch.
Fasten off and sew to chelicerae.

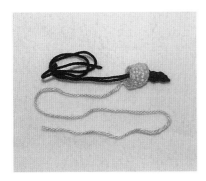

FINISHING

Assemble spider as shown in photo. The sternum
serves as the guide point for attaching the legs; the legs
should butt up against the sternum.

Weave in all ends.

CRICKET

BODY

With tan, begin with a magic loop

Round 1: 5 sc in loop. (5 sts)

Round 2: 2 sc in each st around. (10 sts)

Round 3: *Sc in next st, 2 sc in next st; rep from *
around. (15 sts)

Rounds 4–11: Sc in each st around. (15 sts)

Round 12: *Sc in next st, sc2tog; rep from * around.
(10 sts)

Begin stuffing.

Round 13: Sc2tog around. (5 sts)

Fasten off and sew end together flat.

Embroider details on cricket as shown in photo.

RIGHT LEG

Ch 21. Sc in second ch from hook and in next 5 ch. Sl
st in all remaining chain loops. Fasten off.

LEFT LEG

Ch 21. Sl st in second ch from hook, and in each ch to
end. Ch 1. Working in unused loops on back of
foundation ch, sc in next 6 chs. Fasten off.

FINISHING

Sew legs to cricket. Weave in ends.

If your tarantula is especially hungry, you might need to make extra crickets!

Abbreviations

[ ]	work instructions within brackets as many times as directed
*	repeat the instructions following the single asterisk as directed
* … **	repeat the instructions between the sets of asterisks as many times as directed
beg	beginning
bp	back post (e.g., bpdc, back post double crochet)
CC	contrasting color
ch	chain stitch
ch-	refers to chain or space previously made (e.g., ch-1 space)
ch-sp	chain space
dc	double crochet
dc2tog	double crochet 2 stitches together
dtr	double treble
fp	front post (e.g., fpsc, front post single crochet)
hdc	half double crochet
MC	main color
rem	remaining
rep	repeat
rnd(s)	round(s)
sc	single crochet
sc2tog	single crochet 2 stitches together
sk	skip
sl st	slip stitch
sp(s)	space(s)
st(s)	stitch(es)
tbl	through the back loop
tfl	through the front loop
tog	together
tr	treble crochet
yo	yarn over

Abbreviations are based on those recommended by the Craft Yarn Council; see http://www.craftyarncouncil.com/crochet.html for more information

Yarn Weights

Standard Yarn Weight System

Categories of yarn, gauge ranges, and recommended needle and hook sizes

Yarn Weight Symbol & Category Names	0 Lace	1 Super Fine	2 Fine	3 Light	4 Medium	5 Bulky	6 Super Bulky
Type of Yarns in Category	Fingering 10 count crochet thread	Sock, Fingering, Baby	Sport, Baby	DK, Light Worsted	Worsted, Afghan, Aran	Chunky, Craft, Rug	Bulky, Roving
Knit Gauge Range* in Stockinette Stitch to 4 inches	33 –40** sts	27–32 sts	23–26 sts	21–24 sts	16–20 sts	12–15 sts	6–11 sts
Recommended Needle in Metric Size Range	1.5–2.25 mm	2.25–3.25 mm	3.25–3.75 mm	3.75–4.5 mm	4.5–5.5 mm	5.5–8 mm	8 mm and larger
Recommended Needle U.S. Size Range	000 to 1	1 to 3	3 to 5	5 to 7	7 to 9	9 to 11	11 and larger
Crochet Gauge* Ranges in Single Crochet to 4 inch	32-42 double crochets**	21–32 sts	16–20 sts	12–17 sts	11–14 sts	8–11 sts	5–9 sts
Recommended Hook in Metric Size Range	Steel*** 1.6–1.4mm Regular hook 2.25 mm	2.25–3.5 mm	3.5–4.5 mm	4.5–5.5 mm	5.5–6.5 mm	6.5–9 mm	9 mm and larger
Recommended Hook U.S. Size Range	Steel*** 6, 7, 8 Regular hook B–1	B–1 to E–4	E–4 to 7	7 to I–9	I–9 to K–10½	K–10½ to M–13	M–13 and larger

* GUIDELINES ONLY: The above reflect the most commonly used gauges and needle or hook sizes for specific yarn categories.

** Lace weight yarns are usually knitted or crocheted on larger needles and hooks to create lacy, openwork patterns. Accordingly, a gauge range is difficult to determine. Always follow the gauge stated in your pattern.

*** Steel crochet hooks are sized differently from regular hooks--the higher the number, the smaller the hook, which is the reverse of regular hook sizing.

This Standards & Guidelines booklet and downloadable symbol artwork are available at: **YarnStandards.com**

Visual Index